Mastering the Google Pixel 9a: A Comprehensive Guide for Beginners, Seniors, and First-Time Android Users

Table of contents

Introduction

Overview of the Google Pixel 9a

The Google Pixel 9a is part of Google's flagship Pixel series, offering users a premium smartphone experience with an emphasis on simplicity, quality, and integration with Google's powerful software ecosystem. The Pixel 9a, like its predecessors, continues the trend of blending hardware excellence with exceptional software optimization. It is designed to appeal to users who seek top-tier performance, high-quality photography, and seamless integration with Google services at an affordable price point.

The phone is an ideal option for tech-savvy users and anyone looking to step up their mobile experience without having to break the bank. With its clean Android interface, minimal bloatware, and timely software updates directly from Google, the Pixel 9a provides users with a fast, secure, and reliable smartphone experience.

The Pixel 9a's physical design maintains a sleek, modern look with smooth edges, a balanced weight, and a fingerprint-resistant back panel. The display quality stands out with vibrant colors, and the battery life lasts through daily use without any major concerns. At the heart of the Pixel 9a is its processor, which offers efficient performance for multitasking, gaming, and running intensive applications.

But what truly sets the Pixel 9a apart from its competitors is its camera. Google's image processing technology, coupled with the high-quality lenses, ensures that every photo taken with the Pixel 9a is rich in detail and color, with the company's renowned Night Sight and computational photography enhancing photos in low-light settings. With Google's software-driven focus on camera optimization, users can expect excellent results in nearly every lighting condition.

Furthermore, Google's commitment to privacy and security ensures that Pixel 9a users benefit from advanced security features such as the Titan M security chip, regular security patches, and integrated Google services like Google Assistant. All of these aspects make the Google Pixel 9a a compelling choice for anyone looking for a reliable, secure, and feature-packed smartphone.

Key Features and Specifications

The Google Pixel 9a is packed with features designed to provide users with a smooth and enjoyable mobile experience. Below is a detailed breakdown of the Pixel 9a's key specifications and features.

Display

The Pixel 9a boasts a 6.2-inch Full HD+ OLED display, offering users stunning visuals with rich colors, deep blacks, and crisp details. The OLED technology allows for excellent contrast ratios, making every image, video, or web page pop. Additionally, the display supports HDR content, so users can enjoy compatible streaming services in their best visual form. The screen's 90Hz refresh rate ensures a fluid and responsive experience when scrolling, gaming, or navigating apps.

Processor and Performance

Powered by the Qualcomm Snapdragon 765G chipset, the Pixel 9a strikes a perfect balance between power and energy efficiency. This mid-range processor ensures smooth performance for a variety of tasks, including gaming, multitasking, and media consumption. The GPU integrated within the Snapdragon 765G provides excellent graphics rendering, ensuring a great gaming experience without lag or stuttering.

The device also comes with 6GB of RAM, which allows users to seamlessly switch between apps, run multiple apps simultaneously, and handle demanding tasks with ease.

Camera System

One of the standout features of the Pixel 9a is its advanced camera system, which is powered by Google's computational photography technology. The phone features a 12.2 MP primary camera and a 16 MP ultra-wide lens. The combination of these lenses allows users to capture stunning landscapes, portraits, and close-ups with ease. The camera's Night Sight mode captures clear, detailed images even in low-light conditions, eliminating the need for a flash in most cases.

The front-facing 8 MP camera offers high-quality selfies, while video recording capabilities reach 4K at 30fps, allowing users to capture smooth and vibrant video content.

Battery Life

The Pixel 9a is equipped with a 3,885 mAh battery, which provides all-day battery life under normal usage. Whether you're browsing the web, watching videos, or using social media, the Pixel 9a ensures that you can keep going throughout the day without worrying about running out of power. For users who need even faster charging, the Pixel 9a supports 18W fast charging, ensuring that you can recharge your device quickly when needed.

Operating System and Software

Running on a pure Android experience, the Pixel 9a offers a clean and optimized interface without unnecessary bloatware or third-party customizations. Google's version of Android is known for being user-friendly, fast, and intuitive, and the Pixel 9a delivers this experience at its best. The phone also benefits from Google's software updates directly, ensuring that it receives the latest features and security patches in a timely manner.

Additional Features

- **5G Connectivity:** The Pixel 9a supports 5G, allowing users to enjoy faster download and upload speeds, especially in areas where 5G networks are available.

- **Fingerprint Sensor:** For added security, the Pixel 9a features an under-display fingerprint sensor for quick and secure unlocking of your device.

- **Water Resistance:** With an IP67 rating, the Pixel 9a is resistant to dust and can withstand immersion in water up to 1 meter for 30 minutes.

What's in the Box

When you unbox your Google Pixel 9a, you'll find everything you need to get started right away. Here's a rundown of the items included in the box:

1. **Google Pixel 9a Smartphone** – The main star of the show. The Pixel 9a is sleek, stylish, and ready to be set up.

2. **USB-C to USB-C Cable** – Used for charging the device or transferring data between devices.

3. **18W USB-C Power Adapter** – A fast charger to ensure that your Pixel 9a gets up to speed quickly when it needs a recharge.

4. **SIM Card Ejector Tool** – A small, yet essential tool for inserting or removing the SIM card.

5. **Quick Start Guide** – A simple, easy-to-understand guide to help you set up your Pixel 9a and start using it immediately.

6. **Warranty Card** – A standard card providing information about the warranty coverage for your device.

7. **Safety and Regulatory Information** – Legal documents that explain safety precautions and regulatory compliance.

It's important to note that, as part of Google's ongoing efforts to reduce environmental impact, the Pixel 9a may not come with accessories like a 3.5mm headphone jack adapter, which is a move toward wireless audio solutions. Google promotes wireless audio experiences, including Bluetooth headphones and earbuds, as the future of mobile audio.

Setting Up Your Pixel 9a for the First Time

Getting started with the Google Pixel 9a is simple, and Google makes it a smooth process with clear instructions and a user-friendly setup experience. Follow these steps to get your device up and running:

Step 1: Power On Your Pixel 9a

To begin, press and hold the power button on the right side of the device until the Google logo appears. This signals that your Pixel 9a is powered on and ready for the setup process.

Step 2: Select Your Language and Region

Once the device powers up, you'll be prompted to select your language and region. This ensures that the correct keyboard layout, time zone, and language preferences are set for your device.

Step 3: Connect to Wi-Fi

The next step is to connect to a Wi-Fi network. This allows you to download updates, apps, and set up your Google account. Simply select your network from the list and enter the Wi-Fi password.

Step 4: Sign in to Your Google Account

Signing in to your Google account is an essential step, as it allows you to access Google services like Gmail, Google Photos, Google Drive, and more. If you don't have a Google account, you can create one during the setup process.

Step 5: Restore Your Data (Optional)

If you're upgrading from an older device, you can restore your apps, contacts, and other data from a previous Android phone using Google's easy transfer process. This step helps you quickly get your new Pixel 9a set up with your most-used apps and data.

Step 6: Set Up Security Features

For enhanced security, you'll be prompted to set up a screen lock option (PIN, pattern, or password) and add biometric authentication methods like a fingerprint or face unlock. These features provide added layers of protection for your device.

Step 7: Customize Your Settings

Once the basic setup is complete, you'll be guided through some of the key settings on your Pixel 9a, including display preferences, notifications, privacy settings, and more. Take a moment to personalize your device to your liking.

Step 8: Explore the Pixel Experience

After the setup is complete, you can start exploring the features of your new Pixel 9a. Open the camera app, customize your home screen, and check out some of the helpful Google services that make the Pixel 9a a standout device in the smartphone market.

Chapter 1: Getting Started with Your Google Pixel 9a

Turning Your Device On and Off

Powering On:

To begin using your Google Pixel 9a, locate the power button on the right side of the device. Press and hold this button for a few seconds until the Google logo appears on the screen. This indicates that the device is booting up. Once the home screen appears, your device is ready for use.

Powering Off:

To turn off your Pixel 9a, press and hold the power button until the power menu appears on the screen. You'll see options such as "Power off" and "Restart." Tap on "Power off," and confirm your choice if prompted. Your device will shut down completely.

Restarting Your Device:

If your device is unresponsive or you wish to refresh its performance, restarting can be helpful. Press and hold the power button until the power menu appears, then tap on "Restart." Confirm your choice if prompted, and the device will reboot.

Emergency Restart:

In rare cases where the device becomes unresponsive and the power button doesn't work, you can perform an emergency restart. Press and hold the power button and the volume down button simultaneously for about 10 seconds. The device will force a restart.

Navigating the Home Screen

Understanding the Layout:

The home screen of your Pixel 9a is the central hub for accessing apps, widgets, and settings. At the bottom of the screen, you'll find the navigation bar with icons for "Home," "Back," and "Recent apps." These icons help you navigate through the device efficiently.

Accessing Apps:

To open an app, tap on its icon on the home screen or in the app drawer. The app drawer can be accessed by swiping up from the bottom of the home screen. Here, you'll find all your installed apps organized alphabetically.

Using Widgets:

Widgets are small applications that provide information or quick access to certain features. To add a widget, tap and hold on an empty space on the home screen, then select "Widgets." Browse through the available widgets and drag the one you want to add to your home screen.

Managing Home Screen Pages:

You can have multiple pages on your home screen to organize your apps and widgets. To add a new page, swipe to the far right of your current home screen and tap on the "+" icon. To remove a page, tap and hold on an empty space, then tap on the trash can icon at the top of the screen.

Customizing the Navigation Bar:

If you prefer gesture navigation over the traditional navigation buttons, you can change this in the settings. Go to "Settings" > "System" > "Gestures" > "System navigation," and select your preferred navigation style.

Customizing Your Pixel 9a Settings

Accessing Settings:

To access the settings menu, swipe down from the top of the screen to open the notification shade, then tap on the gear icon. Alternatively, you can find the "Settings" app in your app drawer.

Adjusting Display Settings:

In the settings menu, tap on "Display" to adjust various display options. Here, you can change the brightness level, enable adaptive brightness, adjust the screen timeout duration, and toggle features like Night Light and Dark theme.

Changing Wallpaper:

To personalize your device, you can change the wallpaper. In the "Display" settings, tap on "Wallpaper," then choose from the available options or select an image from your gallery.

Setting Up Do Not Disturb:

To minimize interruptions, you can enable "Do Not Disturb" mode. In the settings menu, tap on "Sound & vibration," then "Do Not Disturb." Here, you can customize which notifications are allowed during this mode.

Managing Notifications:

To manage how notifications appear, go to "Settings" > "Apps & notifications" > "Notifications." Here, you can adjust settings for individual apps, including whether they can send notifications and how they appear.

Connecting to Wi-Fi and Mobile Data

Connecting to Wi-Fi:

To connect to a Wi-Fi network, swipe down from the top of the screen to open the Quick Settings menu. Tap on the Wi-Fi icon to open the Wi-Fi settings. Your device will scan for available networks. Tap on the network you wish to connect to, enter the password if required, and tap "Connect."

Managing Wi-Fi Networks:

To manage saved Wi-Fi networks, go to "Settings" > "Network & internet" > "Wi-Fi." Here, you can see a list of saved networks, forget networks, or add a new network manually.

Connecting to Mobile Data:

To enable mobile data, swipe down from the top of the screen to open the Quick Settings menu. Tap on the mobile data icon to turn it on. To manage mobile data settings, go to "Settings" > "Network & internet" > "Mobile network." Here, you can set data limits, enable data saver, and manage roaming settings.

Switching Between Wi-Fi and Mobile Data:

Your device will automatically switch between Wi-Fi and mobile data based on availability and signal strength. If you prefer to use mobile data over Wi-Fi, you can disable Wi-Fi in the Quick Settings menu.

Setting Up Google Account and Apps

Adding a Google Account:

To add a Google account, go to "Settings" > "Accounts" > "Add account," then select "Google." Follow the on-screen instructions to sign in with your existing Google account or create a new one.

Syncing Google Services:

Once your Google account is added, you can choose which services to sync. Go to "Settings" > "Accounts" > "Google," then select your account. Here, you can toggle the sync options for services like Gmail, Contacts, Calendar, and Drive.

Installing Apps from Google Play Store:

To install apps, open the "Play Store" app from your app drawer. Use the search bar to find the app you want, then tap "Install." Once installed, the app icon will appear on your home screen or in the app drawer.

Managing App Permissions:

To manage app permissions, go to "Settings" > "Apps & notifications" > "App permissions." Here, you can see which apps have access to certain features like location, camera, and microphone, and adjust permissions as needed.

Updating Apps:

To keep your apps up to date, open the "Play Store" app, tap on your profile icon, then tap "Manage apps & device." Here, you can see available updates and tap "Update all" to update all apps at once.

By following these steps, you'll be able to set up and customize your Google Pixel 9a to suit your preferences, ensuring a smooth and enjoyable user experience. If you have any questions or need further assistance, feel free to consult the official Google Pixel support resources or reach out to customer support.

Chapter 2: Essential Features and Functions

Making Calls and Sending Text Messages

The Google Pixel 9a offers an intuitive and streamlined experience when it comes to making calls and sending text messages. Whether you're calling friends and family or sending a quick message to a colleague, your Pixel 9a has you covered.

Making Calls:

To make a call, begin by opening the Phone app on your Pixel 9a. The phone icon is typically located on your home screen or within the app drawer. Once inside the Phone app, you can access your contacts, recent calls, and dialer.

- **Dialing a Number: To** dial a number manually, tap on the dialer icon (the keypad) and enter the phone number. Once the number is entered, tap the green call button to initiate the call.

- **Calling from Contacts**: If you want to call someone from your contacts list, tap on the Contacts tab (usually represented by a person's icon). Scroll through your contacts, select the contact, and tap the call button next to their name.

- **Calling from Recent Calls**: Alternatively, you can make calls directly from your recent calls list, which shows your past calls. Tap on the contact or number, and then tap the call button to place the call.

Managing Calls:

- **Mute and Speakerphone**: During a call, you can enable the speakerphone by tapping the speaker icon. If you need to mute the call, tap the mute icon.

- **Call Waiting and Merging Calls**: If you're on a call and receive another incoming call, you'll hear a beep indicating that there's a second call. You can tap the Add call button to merge calls or Hold to put the current call on hold.

- **Ending a Call:** To end a call, tap the red end call button.

Sending Text Messages:

The process of sending a text message on the Google Pixel 9a is straightforward and intuitive. Use the Messages app to compose and send text messages.

- **Opening Messages**: The Messages app is pre-installed on your Pixel 9a. Open the app from the home screen or app drawer. Once inside, tap on the + (New message) icon to begin a new conversation.
- **Composing a Text:** Enter the recipient's phone number or name if they're in your contacts. Then, tap the text field at the bottom of the screen and start typing your message.
- **Sending Media in a Text:** You can also send photos, videos, or audio files by tapping the attachment icon (paperclip) in the message composition window. You can select images or videos from your gallery or capture new content using the camera.
- **Replying to a Message:** To reply to a message, simply tap on the message thread in your inbox and type your reply. You can also use features like emoji, GIFs, or even voice-to-text for quicker responses.

Organizing Conversations:

Your Pixel 9a offers several features for managing text conversations:
- **Archiving Messages:** To keep your inbox clean, you can archive conversations. Swipe left or right on a conversation thread and tap on the archive icon.
- **Marking Messages as Important**: Mark a message as important by tapping and holding on a message, then selecting star to indicate priority.

Using Google Assistant

Google Assistant is a powerful tool built into your Pixel 9a, offering hands-free control, smart suggestions, and personalized experiences. By simply saying "Hey Google" or "Ok Google," you can issue commands and get answers to almost anything.

Activating Google Assistant:

To activate Google Assistant, either say "Hey Google" or press and hold the home button. This will launch Google Assistant, and you can begin speaking your command or query.

Common Commands and Features:

- **Asking for Information:** Google Assistant can help with a variety of tasks. For example, you can ask it questions like "What's the weather today?" or "What's the score of the game?"
- **Setting Alarms and Reminders:** You can set alarms or reminders by saying "Set an alarm for 7 AM" or "Remind me to call John at 3 PM."
- **Making Calls and Sending Texts:** Simply say, "Call [Contact Name]" or "Text [Contact Name] I'll be there in 10 minutes."
- **Controlling Smart Home Devices**: If you have smart devices set up, you can say things like, "Turn off the lights" or "Set the thermostat to 72 degrees."

- Playing Music and Entertainment: Ask Google Assistant to play your favorite music, movies, or videos by saying things like "Play music by [Artist Name]" or "Play a YouTube video about [Topic]."

Personalization:

Google Assistant can be personalized based on your preferences. You can access your Google Assistant settings through the Google Assistant app or by navigating to Settings > Google > Google Assistant. Here, you can adjust settings related to language preferences, linked accounts, and even voice match to make the assistant more tailored to you.

Setting Up and Managing Notifications

Notifications are an important part of your Pixel 9a experience, as they keep you informed of incoming messages, calls, updates, and other activities. Managing these notifications can improve your user experience by preventing unnecessary distractions.

Managing Notifications:

To view your notifications, swipe down from the top of the screen. Here, you'll see banners for incoming messages, updates, and alerts.

- **Expanding Notifications:** To view more details, swipe down on any notification. You'll be able to read the full message, check emails, or see the entire content of an alert.
- **Clearing Notifications:** To clear individual notifications, swipe them left or right. If you want to clear all notifications, tap the Clear all button at the top of the notification shade.

Customizing Notifications:

Your Pixel 9a offers detailed options for customizing notifications:
- **Do Not Disturb Mode:** To enable Do Not Disturb, swipe down from the top of the screen and tap on the Do Not Disturb icon. You can customize the settings in Settings > Sound & Vibration > Do Not Disturb to allow only certain notifications.
- **Notification Settings by App**: To manage how specific apps send notifications, go to Settings > Apps & Notifications > Notifications, then select the app. From here, you can choose to block or adjust the notification style for each app.
- **Notification Priority:** For important apps like messaging or email, you can adjust their notification priority to ensure they appear at the top of your notifications list.

Managing Battery Life and Power Saving Tips

The Google Pixel 9a comes equipped with a long-lasting battery, but managing its life is key to ensuring optimal performance throughout the day.

Battery Settings and Usage:

To check your battery usage and settings, go to Settings > Battery. Here, you'll find a breakdown of how much battery each app is consuming. You can tap on any app to see more detailed information.

- **Battery Percentage:** To enable the battery percentage icon in the status bar, go to Settings > Battery and toggle on Battery percentage.
- **Battery Saver Mode: If** you need to conserve battery, enable Battery Saver mode. Go to Settings > Battery > Battery Saver, and toggle it on. This will limit background processes and notifications to extend battery life.

Adaptive Battery:

Your Pixel 9a comes with Adaptive Battery, a feature that learns your usage patterns and prioritizes power for apps that you use most frequently. To enable it, go to Settings > Battery > Adaptive Battery.

Power Saving Tips:

- **Dim the Screen**: Lowering your screen brightness or enabling adaptive brightness can significantly reduce battery drain.
- **Turn Off Unnecessary Features:** Disable features like Bluetooth and Location services when not in use.
- **Disable Background Apps:** Close apps running in the background by swiping up on the app tray and removing them. This prevents apps from using excessive power.

Using the Lock Screen and Security Features

The lock screen is a crucial element of your Pixel 9a's security, and setting it up correctly ensures your device stays safe from unauthorized access.

Setting Up the Lock Screen:

To set up a lock screen, go to Settings > Security > Screen lock. From here, you can choose between several types of locks:
- **Pattern Lock:** Draw a pattern on the screen to unlock your phone.
- **PIN Lock:** Enter a numeric PIN to unlock your device.
- **Password**: Use a more complex alphanumeric password.
- **Fingerprint:** Set up a fingerprint scan for a more secure and quick unlock method. This can be enabled in Settings > Security > Fingerprint.

Using Face Unlock:

If you prefer, you can also use Face Unlock for a more convenient unlocking option. Go to Settings > Security > Face Unlock to set it up.

Securing Your Google Account:

Your Google account is a crucial part of your security. To ensure it is secure, enable two-factor authentication (2FA). This adds an extra layer of security by requiring a second verification step when signing in to your account.

Find My Device:

Google's Find My Device feature allows you to locate your Pixel 9a in case it's lost or stolen. Go to Settings >

Security > Find My Device to enable this feature. You can access Find My Device from any web browser by visiting the Google website and signing into your Google account.

With these essential features and functions, the Google Pixel 9a ensures that you're fully equipped to make the most out of your device. By managing calls, text messages, notifications, battery life, and security features, you can tailor your phone experience to meet your needs while keeping your data and information safe.

Chapter 3: Camera and Photography

The Google Pixel 9a comes equipped with a state-of-the-art camera system designed to provide outstanding photo and video quality, even for users who are new to photography. Whether you're capturing everyday moments or taking photos in challenging lighting, the Pixel 9a's camera is built to deliver beautiful, clear, and crisp results. In this chapter, we'll dive deep into the camera features, explaining everything from basic usage to advanced functions like Night Sight and Google Photos storage.

Introduction to the Google Pixel 9a Camera

The Google Pixel 9a's camera system features an advanced, AI-driven setup that allows for incredible photos and videos, even in less-than-ideal lighting conditions. The combination of cutting-edge technology and simple, user-friendly features makes it easy for anyone to take stunning photos with little to no effort.

Key Features of the Google Pixel 9a Camera:

- **12.2 MP Dual-Pixel Main Camera**: The primary camera is designed to capture sharp, high-resolution images. With Dual-Pixel autofocus, the Pixel 9a offers incredibly fast and accurate focusing.

- **8 MP Front-Facing Camera**: Ideal for selfies, video calls, and group shots. The front camera also supports Portrait Mode for beautiful, bokeh-filled photos.

- **HDR+ and Computational Photography**: The Pixel 9a utilizes Google's HDR+ technology, which enhances the dynamic range in photos, ensuring that both bright and dark areas are well-exposed. This is especially useful in high-contrast situations like sunset or night photography.

- **Wide Angle Lens**: For capturing sweeping landscapes or large group photos, the Pixel 9a includes a wide-angle lens that enables a broader field of view, ensuring you can fit more into your frame without having to step back.

- **Video Capabilities**: The camera supports 4K video recording at 30fps and 1080p at 60fps, allowing you to record in high-definition quality for both personal projects and professional use.

Using the Camera App: To start taking photos with your Pixel 9a, simply open the **Camera app**. You can find it on your home screen or in the app drawer. The interface is clean and minimalist, with easy-to-use controls that allow even beginners to start snapping high-quality photos right away.

The **shutter button** is positioned at the bottom of the screen for easy access, while additional features like flash settings, switching between the front and rear cameras, and toggling between photo and video modes are accessible via intuitive icons.

Capturing Stunning Photos and Videos

Capturing high-quality photos with the Google Pixel 9a is incredibly easy, thanks to its robust camera system. The following tips will help you get the most out of your photos and videos.

1. Taking Photos with the Main Camera:

- **Basic Photography**: Open the Camera app and ensure you're in **Photo Mode** (the default setting). Frame your shot, tap the **shutter**

button to take the photo, and voila—your Pixel 9a will handle the rest. The camera's AI will optimize the shot, adjusting exposure, color balance, and sharpness to create a stunning image.

- **Portrait Mode**: Portrait mode allows you to take photos with a blurred background, emphasizing the subject of your photo. This mode is especially useful for portraits, pets, or any subject you want to stand out. You can switch to Portrait Mode by swiping to the **Portrait** tab in the camera app, then tapping the shutter when you're ready to snap the photo. The Pixel 9a's AI will create a natural-looking bokeh effect for a professional touch.

- **Wide-Angle Lens**: To capture more in your shot, especially in tight spaces or landscapes, swipe to the **Wide-Angle** mode. This setting lets you include more of the scene without needing to step back.

2. Taking Videos with the Google Pixel 9a:

- **Video Mode**: To switch to video mode, swipe to the **Video** tab in the camera app. Tap the **record button** to start recording. You can also toggle between **standard video** and **slow**

motion by selecting the corresponding icon.

- **Stabilization**: The Pixel 9a has built-in video stabilization, which helps smooth out your recordings and reduce shaky footage when walking or moving. If you're recording in 4K, it's especially important to keep your movements steady to capture smooth footage.

3. Capturing Motion with Top Shot:

Top Shot is a smart feature that uses AI to automatically capture the best moment during a photo or video. When you take a picture, the camera will recommend the best shot by analyzing your photos and selecting the one with the least amount of blur, the best expressions, and the sharpest details. To activate Top Shot, simply open the camera, frame your shot, and press the shutter. Once you review your photo, Google will automatically suggest the best moment from the sequence.

Using Night Sight and Other Camera Modes

One of the standout features of the Google Pixel 9a is its **Night Sight** mode, which allows you to capture stunning photos even in low-light environments.

1. Night Sight:

Night Sight is designed to produce clear, detailed photos in low-light conditions. Whether you're taking photos indoors at night, outside under dim streetlights, or in any environment with minimal light, Night Sight helps you achieve beautiful, well-exposed images.

To activate Night Sight:

- Open the **Camera app**.

- Swipe to **Night Sight** from the bottom menu.

- Aim your camera at the scene you want to capture.

- Hold your phone steady while the camera captures multiple frames and uses AI to process the image.

Night Sight also automatically adjusts the shutter speed and ISO to capture as much light as possible, resulting in images that are bright, clear, and rich in detail. You no longer need to worry about blurry, grainy photos in dark settings.

2. Other Camera Modes:

Besides Night Sight, the Pixel 9a comes with several other useful camera modes that can enhance your photography experience:

- **Portrait Mode**: As mentioned earlier, this mode creates a depth-of-field effect that blurs the background while keeping the subject sharp. Ideal for portraits, pets, or still-life photography.

- **Panorama Mode**: If you're capturing a vast landscape, the **Panorama** mode allows you to slowly move the camera across a scene to take wide-angle photos that capture more detail.

- **Lens Blur**: For a more dramatic blurred background effect, **Lens Blur** mode is a great option. This feature mimics the effect produced by professional cameras with a wide aperture lens.

- **Time-Lapse Mode**: For capturing scenes that change slowly over time, like sunsets or city traffic, use **Time-Lapse**. This mode speeds up the footage to create a compressed video that's both entertaining and dynamic.

- **Slow Motion**: If you're capturing fast-moving action, **Slow Motion** allows you to record in slow motion, highlighting details you might miss with the naked eye.

Editing and Sharing Your Photos

Once you've captured the perfect photo or video, you'll likely want to edit and share it with others. The Google Pixel 9a provides several built-in editing tools, making it easy to enhance your images directly from the camera app.

1. Editing Photos:

The **Google Photos app** offers a range of powerful editing tools that allow you to fine-tune your photos. Here are some of the basic editing features:

- **Crop and Rotate**: You can crop your image to improve the composition or rotate it if you've captured it in the wrong orientation.

- **Filters**: Google Photos comes with a variety of filters that can help enhance the mood or style of your photos.

- **Adjustments**: Use the **adjustment sliders** to control elements like brightness, contrast, saturation, shadows, and highlights. These fine-tuning tools help you achieve the perfect look for your image.

- **Healing Tool**: The **healing tool** allows you to remove unwanted objects from your photos. This tool works by intelligently filling in the background behind the object you want to remove.

- **Portrait Light**: This tool simulates the effect of studio lighting, giving your portraits a more professional finish.

2. Sharing Photos:

Sharing photos with friends and family is easy on the Google Pixel 9a. From Google Photos, you can share directly to social media platforms, email, or even text messages. Simply open the photo you want to share, tap the **share icon** (usually represented by three connected dots), and select how you'd like to share the image.

Additionally, if you have Google Photos set to automatically back up your photos, you can share albums, collaborate with others on shared albums, and even create and share **photo books** or **collages**.

Using Google Photos for Storage and Backup

Google Photos provides unlimited cloud storage for high-quality photos and videos, making it easy to back up all of your memories securely.

1. Setting Up Google Photos:

To get started with Google Photos, make sure the app is installed on your Pixel 9a. Open the app, and it will prompt you to sign in with your Google account. Once signed in, Google Photos will automatically sync your photos and videos to the cloud, ensuring they're safely backed up.

2. Managing Your Photos in Google Photos:

Google Photos offers powerful search capabilities, enabling you to quickly find photos based on objects, people, locations, or even text within the image. You can also organize your photos into albums, allowing for easy access to specific sets of images.

3. Free Up Space:

If you're running low on storage, Google Photos can help by offering the option to delete photos that have already been backed up. Simply go to **Settings** > **Free up space** and Google Photos will remove local copies of your photos while keeping them safely stored in the cloud.

The Google Pixel 9a's camera is a powerful tool that, with a little guidance, will help you take beautiful, professional-quality photos. Whether you're an amateur photographer or an experienced shutterbug, the intuitive interface and advanced features make it easy to capture stunning photos and videos in any situation.

Chapter 4: Apps and Services

The Google Pixel 9a is designed to provide a seamless, intuitive experience, and much of that experience revolves around apps and services. From productivity tools like Gmail and Google Calendar to entertainment apps and social media, the Pixel 9a offers easy access to the world of apps. In this chapter, we'll walk you through installing and managing apps, exploring preinstalled features, and customizing app permissions and notifications to tailor your device to your needs.

Installing and Managing Apps from the Google Play Store

One of the key features of the Pixel 9a is its access to the **Google Play Store**, which is home to millions of apps, games, movies, books, and more. Installing apps on your Pixel 9a is a simple process, and managing them is just as easy. Whether you're looking for productivity tools, entertainment, or specialized apps, the Play Store has everything you need.

Installing Apps from the Google Play Store

To install apps from the Google Play Store:

1. **Open the Google Play Store**: From your home screen, locate and open the **Google Play Store** app. It's easily identifiable with the colorful triangle logo.

2. **Search for Apps**: At the top of the Play Store, you'll see a **search bar**. You can type the name of the app you want to install, or you can browse through categories like **Games**, **Top Charts**, **Categories**, or **Editor's Choice** to discover new apps.

3. **Select an App**: Once you've found an app, tap on it to open the app's page. Here you can see details about the app, including screenshots, user reviews, and app permissions.

4. **Install the App**: If you decide to install the app, simply tap the **Install** button. For paid apps, you'll see the price, and you'll be prompted to complete your purchase.

5. **Wait for the Download to Complete**: Once the app starts downloading, it will be automatically installed on your Pixel 9a. The progress of the download will be displayed at the top of your screen. Once the app is installed,

you'll see an **Open** button, which you can tap to launch the app.

Managing Installed Apps

Once apps are installed, it's important to know how to manage them for an optimal experience. You can update, uninstall, or change the settings of your apps whenever you like.

- **Updating Apps**: The Google Play Store will notify you when updates are available for your installed apps. You can update individual apps by going to the **My Apps & Games** section of the Play Store or update all apps by tapping the **Update All** button.

- **Uninstalling Apps**: If you want to free up storage space or remove an app you no longer use, you can easily uninstall it. To do so, go to **Settings > Apps & Notifications**, select the app you want to remove, and tap **Uninstall**.

- **App Settings**: For each installed app, you can manage specific settings such as notifications, permissions, and data usage by going to **Settings > Apps & Notifications > See All Apps**. Here you can tap on any app to customize its settings.

Preinstalled Apps and Features

Your Google Pixel 9a comes with several preinstalled apps and features that are designed to enhance your experience, streamline your tasks, and provide essential tools for everyday use. These apps are a significant part of the Google ecosystem, allowing you to stay connected, productive, and entertained.

Key Preinstalled Apps on the Pixel 9a

- **Google Play Store**: As discussed earlier, the Play Store is where you download and manage all apps. It's the gateway to millions of apps, games, movies, and more.

- **Gmail**: Gmail is the default email app on the Pixel 9a, providing easy access to your inbox and Google's powerful email features. The app supports multiple accounts, automatic sorting of important emails, and integration with Google's other services like Calendar and Drive.

- **Google Calendar**: The Google Calendar app helps you keep track of appointments, meetings, events, and reminders. You can integrate it with Gmail for automatic event creation and sync it across all your devices, ensuring you never miss an important date.

- **Google Drive**: Google Drive is a cloud storage service that allows you to store your documents, photos, videos, and other files. It comes with 15GB of free storage and seamlessly integrates with other Google services. You can upload files, create documents and spreadsheets with Google Docs, Sheets, and Slides, and share your files with others.

- **Google Photos**: With **Google Photos**, you can store and manage your photos and videos. Google Photos offers unlimited storage for photos (up to 16MP) and videos (up to 1080p), making it easy to backup your media and access it from any device. The app also includes intelligent search capabilities, automatic photo enhancements, and a host of editing tools.

- **Google Maps**: Google Maps is one of the most comprehensive navigation apps available. It helps you find directions, explore new places, and even get real-time traffic updates. Google Maps also integrates with other Google services, such as Google Assistant and Google Street View, for a more personalized experience.

- **Google Assistant**: Google Assistant is your virtual assistant on the Pixel 9a. It allows you to use voice commands to perform various tasks, such as sending messages, making calls, setting reminders, checking the weather, and even controlling smart home devices. You can activate it by saying "Hey Google" or by pressing and holding the home button.

- **YouTube**: The Pixel 9a comes with the YouTube app, allowing you to watch, like, comment, and share videos. You can also upload your own content and manage your YouTube account directly from the app.

- **Messages**: The **Messages** app is the default SMS and MMS messaging app on the Pixel 9a. It allows you to send and receive text messages, share multimedia content, and chat with friends and family. The app also supports **RCS (Rich Communication Services)**, which allows for enhanced messaging features, such as read receipts and typing indicators, as long as both users are using a compatible device.

- **Google Keep**: Google Keep is a note-taking and task management app that allows you to jot down ideas, create to-do lists, and set reminders. Notes are stored in the cloud and sync across all devices that use your Google account.

- **Google Chrome**: Chrome is the default web browser on the Pixel 9a. It offers fast browsing, syncing across devices, and access to a wide range of extensions and features like **Incognito**

Mode for private browsing.

- **Google News**: Stay up-to-date with the latest headlines and breaking news with the **Google News** app. It offers personalized news recommendations, and you can explore stories based on your interests and preferences.

- **Clock**: The **Clock** app helps you keep track of time, set alarms, use a stopwatch, and check the world clock. You can also set up bedtime reminders and use the app to help improve your sleep hygiene.

Using Google Services: Gmail, Calendar, Drive, and More

One of the main reasons for using a Google Pixel device is the seamless integration with Google's suite of services. These services are designed to make your life easier, from managing your email and calendar to organizing your files and documents.

Gmail: Your Email Hub

Gmail is the default email service on the Pixel 9a, and it integrates well with other Google services like **Google Drive**, **Google Calendar**, and **Google Meet**. Gmail offers a clean, user-friendly interface, with powerful tools for sorting emails and customizing your inbox. You can use labels, filters, and folders to manage your messages and ensure that important emails don't get lost.

- **Managing Multiple Accounts**: If you have multiple Gmail accounts, the Pixel 9a allows you to easily switch between them. You can add personal, work, or school accounts and manage them from within the app.

- **Email Notifications**: Customize your notifications to receive alerts for only the most important emails. You can set up different notification settings for each account or for specific labels or folders.

Google Calendar: Organize Your Schedule

Google Calendar is perfect for organizing appointments, meetings, and events. The app syncs across devices, so you'll always have your schedule at hand, no matter where you are.

- **Creating Events**: You can quickly create events by tapping the **plus icon** and adding event details. You can also invite others to your events by entering their email addresses, making it perfect for organizing group activities or work meetings.

- **Syncing with Gmail**: Google Calendar automatically integrates with Gmail to create events from email invitations, such as flight bookings, hotel reservations, and even concert tickets.

Google Drive: Store and Share Files

Google Drive offers cloud storage that allows you to store documents, photos, and videos safely in the cloud. You get 15GB of free storage, and you can purchase more storage if needed.

- **Collaborative Features**: You can create and edit Google Docs, Sheets, and Slides directly in Drive. These documents are automatically saved and synced across all your devices, allowing for real-time collaboration with colleagues or friends.

- **File Sharing**: Drive allows you to share files and folders with others, whether you're working on a project or simply sharing photos or videos with friends.

Google Keep: Capture Ideas and To-Do Lists

Google Keep is a lightweight note-taking app that helps you keep track of your ideas and tasks. Whether you're capturing fleeting thoughts or making detailed lists, Keep is perfect for jotting down quick notes.

- **Sharing Notes**: You can share your notes with others, making it easy to collaborate on projects or keep family members updated on to-do lists.

Customizing App Permissions and Notifications

Your Pixel 9a gives you full control over how apps interact with your data and how they notify you. Customizing app permissions and notifications is essential to ensure your privacy and to maintain a clutter-free notification panel.

App Permissions

To control app permissions:

1. Go to **Settings** > **Apps & Notifications**.

2. Select **See All Apps** and choose an app from the list.

3. Tap **Permissions** to view and manage which permissions the app has. Here you can allow or deny permissions like camera access, location services, and more.

App Notifications

To manage notifications for apps:

1. Go to **Settings** > **Apps & Notifications** > **Notifications**.

2. Choose **See All Apps**, then select an app.

3. Toggle the switch to allow or block notifications. You can also customize notification types, like sound, vibration, and visual alerts.

In this chapter, we've covered how to install and manage apps, explore preinstalled services like Gmail, Calendar, and Drive, and customize app settings to suit your needs. By understanding and optimizing these features, you can maximize the functionality of your Google Pixel 9a and enjoy a truly personalized experience.

Chapter 5: Connectivity and Network Settings

In today's fast-paced digital world, reliable connectivity is more essential than ever. Whether you're browsing the internet, sharing files, or staying connected with loved ones and colleagues, your device's connectivity features play a crucial role. The **Google Pixel 9a** offers a variety of ways to manage mobile data, set up network connections, and interact with other devices, all with user-friendly tools designed for optimal performance. In this chapter, we will dive deep into these features to ensure you get the most out of your Pixel 9a's connectivity and network settings.

Managing Mobile Data and Network Settings

The **mobile data** feature on your Pixel 9a allows you to stay connected to the internet without relying on Wi-Fi. Managing your mobile data usage efficiently is essential to avoid excessive data charges, especially if you have a limited data plan. The Pixel 9a offers several options to help you manage mobile data, including setting data limits, monitoring usage, and optimizing data settings for the best performance.

Turning Mobile Data On or Off

To turn your mobile data on or off:

1. **Swipe Down** from the top of the screen to open the notification shade.

2. Look for the **Mobile Data** icon (it may show as "LTE," "5G," or a similar term depending on your network).

3. Tap the **Mobile Data icon** to toggle it on or off.

Alternatively, you can access the mobile data settings directly through:

1. **Settings > Network & Internet > Mobile Network**.

2. From here, you can toggle mobile data on or off.

Data Usage Settings

To monitor and manage your mobile data usage:

1. Go to **Settings > Network & Internet > Data Usage**.

2. Here, you can view the total amount of data you've used within a set period and see a

breakdown by app.

If you have a data limit on your plan, you can set a **data warning** or **data limit** to avoid going over your monthly allowance. To do this:

1. Tap on **Data warning & limit**.

2. Set a **warning limit** (this will alert you when you're approaching the limit) and a **data limit** (this will automatically disable data once the limit is reached).

Network Settings

Your Pixel 9a supports multiple network types, including **5G**, **4G LTE**, and **3G**, depending on your carrier and location. To select a preferred network:

1. Go to **Settings** > **Network & Internet** > **Mobile Network**.

2. Under **Preferred Network Type**, select the network that best suits your needs, such as **5G**, **4G LTE**, or **3G**.

If you're experiencing slower speeds or connection issues, switching to a lower network type like 4G LTE might help with stability.

Data Saver Mode

For users who want to limit data usage, the **Data Saver mode** can be helpful. It restricts background data usage for apps and reduces data consumption when you're using mobile data. To enable Data Saver:

1. Go to **Settings** > **Network & Internet** > **Data Saver**.

2. Toggle the switch to **On**.

This feature ensures that apps won't use mobile data in the background unless absolutely necessary, helping you conserve data.

Bluetooth, NFC, and Other Connectivity Options

The Google Pixel 9a offers several options for connecting to other devices, including **Bluetooth**, **NFC (Near Field Communication)**, and other wireless features like **Wi-Fi Direct** and **Cast**. Let's explore these features and how you can use them to connect and share data seamlessly.

Bluetooth Connectivity

Bluetooth is an essential tool for connecting wirelessly to a variety of devices, such as headphones, speakers, smartwatches, and more. Here's how to manage Bluetooth connections on your Pixel 9a:

1. **Turn Bluetooth On**: Swipe down from the top of the screen and tap the **Bluetooth** icon to enable Bluetooth. Alternatively, go to **Settings > Connected Devices > Bluetooth**.

2. **Pairing Devices**: To pair a new device, tap on **Pair New Device** under Bluetooth settings. The Pixel 9a will search for nearby devices in pairing mode. Once the device appears in the list, tap on it to pair.

3. **Managing Paired Devices**: Once paired, the device will appear in your Bluetooth settings under **Previously Connected Devices**. From here, you can tap on any device to manage settings like renaming the device, disconnecting it, or unpairing it.

NFC (Near Field Communication)

NFC allows for quick, short-range communication between devices. It's commonly used for tasks like **contactless payments, data transfer**, and **pairing devices**.

To enable NFC:

1. Go to **Settings** > **Connected Devices** > **Connection Preferences** > **NFC**.

2. Toggle the switch to turn NFC on.

Once enabled, you can use NFC for various tasks like:

- **Contactless payments** with **Google Pay** by tapping your Pixel 9a on an NFC-enabled payment terminal.

- **Data transfer** by placing two NFC-enabled devices back to back to transfer files like photos or contacts.

- **Pairing Bluetooth devices** more quickly by tapping your phone to the other device's NFC tag.

Wi-Fi Direct and Wi-Fi Hotspot

The **Wi-Fi Direct** feature allows your Pixel 9a to connect directly to other devices over Wi-Fi without needing a router. This is particularly useful for file transfers or screen sharing.

To use **Wi-Fi Direct**:

1. Open **Settings** > **Network & Internet** > **Wi-Fi** > **Wi-Fi Preferences**.

2. Select **Wi-Fi Direct**, and your phone will search for nearby Wi-Fi Direct-enabled devices.

Wi-Fi Hotspot is another feature that lets you share your mobile data connection with other devices, such as tablets or laptops, by turning your Pixel 9a into a Wi-Fi router.

To enable the **Wi-Fi Hotspot**:

1. Go to **Settings** > **Network & Internet** > **Hotspot & Tethering**.

2. Toggle on **Wi-Fi Hotspot**.

3. Configure your hotspot by setting a name and password.

Other devices can now connect to your Pixel 9a's hotspot just like any other Wi-Fi network.

Setting Up Hotspot and Tethering

In addition to Wi-Fi and Bluetooth, your Pixel 9a supports **Tethering** through both **USB** and **Bluetooth** connections. This allows you to share your mobile data with another device that may not have its own internet connection.

Using USB Tethering

USB tethering is useful if you want to share your mobile data connection with a laptop or computer via a USB cable. To set up USB tethering:

1. Connect your Pixel 9a to the other device using a **USB cable**.

2. On your Pixel 9a, go to **Settings** > **Network & Internet** > **Hotspot & Tethering**.

3. Toggle on **USB Tethering**.

Your device will now be able to use your Pixel 9a's mobile data connection for internet access.

Using Bluetooth Tethering

To share your mobile data connection via Bluetooth:

1. Pair your Pixel 9a with the device you want to share the data with, using Bluetooth (as discussed above).

2. Go to **Settings** > **Network & Internet** > **Hotspot & Tethering**.

3. Toggle on **Bluetooth Tethering**.

Once Bluetooth tethering is enabled, the paired device can use your mobile data for internet access.

Connecting to Devices via USB and Wireless

The Pixel 9a offers several ways to connect to other devices through **USB** and **wireless** methods, including using **USB cables** for file transfers or connecting to a computer, and **wireless screen casting**.

Connecting to a Computer via USB

To transfer files between your Pixel 9a and a computer:

1. Connect your phone to the computer using a USB cable.

2. On your Pixel 9a, swipe down the notification shade and tap on the **USB charging this device** notification.

3. Select **File Transfer** or **MTP** from the options that appear.

Your computer should now recognize your Pixel 9a as a media device, allowing you to transfer files like photos, videos, and documents between the two.

Casting to a TV or Other Devices Wirelessly

The Pixel 9a also supports **Google Cast** for wirelessly casting your phone's screen to compatible devices like smart TVs, speakers, or other Chromecast-enabled devices.

1. Ensure that your Pixel 9a and the casting device are on the same Wi-Fi network.

2. Open the **Quick Settings** menu by swiping down from the top of the screen.

3. Tap the **Cast** icon.

4. Select the device you want to cast to, and your screen will be mirrored on the TV or device.

This feature is great for streaming movies, sharing photos, or presenting content during meetings or events.

Conclusion

In this chapter, we've explored how to manage mobile data, network settings, Bluetooth and NFC connectivity, and how to set up hotspot and tethering on your Google Pixel 9a. With these tools, you can optimize your connectivity, share your mobile data with others, and connect seamlessly to a variety of devices. Whether you're transferring files via USB, casting your screen wirelessly, or managing your mobile data efficiently, the Pixel 9a ensures you stay connected and in control of your network settings.

Chapter 6: Storage and File Management

Your **Google Pixel 9a** provides a range of tools for managing storage, files, and media. As mobile phones become central hubs for data storage, it's crucial to know how to optimize and organize your files efficiently to ensure that you have easy access to them whenever needed. This chapter will guide you through managing internal storage, using Google Drive and other cloud storage services, transferring files between devices, and organizing files and media for easy access.

Managing Internal Storage and Files

The **internal storage** of your Google Pixel 9a is where all your apps, media, and files are saved. While the Pixel 9a comes with a generous amount of storage, it's important to regularly manage it to avoid running out of space. Keeping your storage organized also ensures that you can always access your important files quickly and efficiently.

Checking Available Storage

Before you begin managing your storage, it's a good idea to check how much space you have left. Here's how you can do that:

1. Open **Settings** on your Pixel 9a.

2. Scroll down and select **Storage**.

3. Here, you'll see a breakdown of your storage usage, with categories like **Apps**, **Images**, **Videos**, **Audio**, and **Downloads**.

By looking at this overview, you can identify what types of files are using up the most space and plan accordingly.

Managing and Deleting Files

If you notice that your storage is getting full, it's time to clean up and delete unnecessary files. Here's how you can manage your storage efficiently:

1. **Uninstall Unused Apps**: Go to **Settings > Apps & Notifications > See All Apps**. Here, you can scroll through your apps and uninstall the ones you no longer use. Tap on an app to see details, and select **Uninstall** to free up space.

2. **Delete Old Photos and Videos**: Photos and videos tend to take up a significant portion of your storage. Open the **Photos** app, and start deleting old images or videos you no longer need. Google Photos offers an option to automatically back up your media to the cloud, so you don't lose any memories while freeing up space.

3. **Clear Cache**: Apps often store cached data to improve performance. Over time, this can accumulate and take up valuable storage. To clear the cache:

    ○ Go to **Settings** > **Storage** > **Cached Data**.

    ○ Tap to clear the cache for apps, or do so individually for each app by going to **Settings** > **Apps & Notifications** > **See All Apps** > [App Name] > **Storage** > **Clear Cache**.

4. **Use Smart Storage**: The Pixel 9a offers a feature called **Smart Storage** that automatically deletes photos and videos that have already been backed up to Google Photos. To enable Smart Storage:

    ○ Go to **Settings** > **Storage**.

- Toggle on **Smart Storage**. This will ensure that old photos and videos are removed from your phone after they've been safely backed up.

5. **Manage Downloads**: If you've downloaded files over time, they may start to accumulate and take up space. To review and delete unnecessary downloads, go to the **Files** app, navigate to **Downloads**, and delete any files you no longer need.

Using an SD Card (if applicable)

While the Pixel 9a doesn't have an SD card slot, users who own other Android devices with expandable storage can store files on an SD card to free up internal space. For Pixel users, however, relying on cloud storage and external drives is the best alternative.

Using Google Drive and Cloud Storage

One of the easiest and most efficient ways to manage storage is by using **cloud storage services** like **Google Drive**. Google Drive offers **15GB of free cloud storage**, which can be used for storing documents, photos, videos, and other important files. It also integrates seamlessly with your Google Pixel 9a, allowing for automatic backups of apps and data.

Setting Up Google Drive

To set up Google Drive on your Pixel 9a:

1. Open the **Google Drive** app. If it's not already installed, you can download it from the **Google Play Store**.

2. Sign in using your **Google Account**.

3. Once signed in, you can upload files from your device by tapping the "+" button, then selecting **Upload**. Choose the file you want to upload from your phone.

You can upload **documents, photos, videos, and audio files**, and organize them into folders for easy access. Uploading files to Google Drive ensures they are backed up and accessible from any device.

Automatic Backup with Google Photos

Google Photos offers unlimited cloud storage for photos and videos (with some restrictions on quality), allowing you to free up space on your Pixel 9a while keeping your media safe. To enable automatic backup:

1. Open the **Google Photos** app.

2. Sign in with your Google Account.

3. Go to **Settings** > **Backup & Sync**, and toggle it on.

Once enabled, any photos or videos you take with your Pixel 9a will automatically be backed up to the cloud. If you're running low on storage, you can delete local copies of media from your device while keeping them safely stored in Google Photos.

Sharing Files from Google Drive

Google Drive also allows for easy sharing of files with others. You can share photos, documents, and videos directly from Google Drive. To share a file:

1. Open the **Google Drive** app.

2. Tap on the file you want to share.

3. Select the **Share** icon (three dots or a share symbol).

4. Enter the email address of the person you want to share with or select a contact from your list.

Google Drive also supports file collaboration, allowing multiple people to edit documents, spreadsheets, and slideshows in real time.

Transferring Files Between Devices

Whether you're moving files from your Pixel 9a to your computer, another mobile device, or an external hard drive, file transfer is an essential feature that allows you to easily share and access your data.

Using USB Cable for File Transfer

To transfer files between your Pixel 9a and a computer:

1. Connect your Pixel 9a to your computer using a **USB cable**.

2. On your Pixel 9a, swipe down the notification shade and tap the **USB charging this device** notification.

3. Select **File Transfer** or **MTP** (Media Transfer Protocol) from the options that appear.

4. Your computer will recognize your phone as a storage device, and you can now drag and drop files between your computer and Pixel 9a.

Using Bluetooth for File Transfer

For smaller files or when you don't have a USB cable handy, **Bluetooth** provides a wireless solution for file transfers. To send a file via Bluetooth:

1. Ensure that Bluetooth is turned on both on your Pixel 9a and the receiving device.

2. Pair the devices if they are not already connected.

3. Navigate to the file you wish to send (e.g., a photo in **Google Photos** or a document in **Google Drive**).

4. Tap the **Share** icon and select **Bluetooth** as the sharing method.

5. Select the paired device, and the file will be sent.

Using Google Drive for Cloud-Based File Transfer

For larger files, or to avoid using Bluetooth or cables, you can upload files to **Google Drive** and then download them on another device. This is especially useful for cross-platform file sharing between Android and iOS devices, or between a phone and a computer.

To upload a file:

1. Open **Google Drive** and tap the "+" icon to upload the file.

2. Once uploaded, you can access it from any device that has access to your Google Drive account.

Organizing Files and Media for Easy Access

A well-organized file system ensures that you can find what you need quickly, saving you time and frustration. Here are some tips for organizing your files and media on your Pixel 9a:

Creating Folders

In both the **Files** app and **Google Drive**, you can create folders to group similar files together. For example, you might create a folder for **Work Documents**, **Vacation Photos**, or **Music**. To create a new folder in the **Files** app:

1. Open the **Files** app.

2. Tap the **three dots** in the top-right corner, and select **Create Folder**.

3. Name the folder, and tap **Create**.

You can move files into these folders by selecting them and choosing the **Move** option.

Using Labels in Google Drive

Google Drive allows you to organize your documents with labels. To organize documents by labels:

1. In **Google Drive**, open the document or file.

2. Tap the **three dots** next to the file name, then select **Add Label**.

3. Choose or create a new label, such as **Important** or **Work**.

Using labels in Google Drive makes it easy to group and access similar files, even if they're stored in different folders.

Conclusion

Managing storage, transferring files, and organizing media on your **Google Pixel 9a** is easier than ever with the tools and features provided. By effectively using Google Drive and cloud storage, organizing your files into folders, and transferring data between devices, you can keep your Pixel 9a running smoothly without worrying about running out of space. Whether you're freeing up storage on your device or backing up important documents and media to the cloud, taking the time to properly manage your storage will ensure that you always have access to the files and data that matter most to you.

Chapter 7: Display, Audio, and Visual Settings

Your Google Pixel 9a is designed to deliver an optimal visual and auditory experience. Whether you're watching a movie, playing a game, or reading an article, ensuring that your device is set up with the perfect display and audio settings can make all the difference. This chapter will guide you through adjusting display brightness and resolution, setting up dark mode and themes, managing audio and volume settings, and using screen and sound enhancements to create the best possible viewing and listening experience.

Adjusting Display Brightness and Resolution

The display on the Google Pixel 9a is one of the most important aspects of the device, as it's where you interact with all your apps, media, and content. Whether you're outdoors under bright sunlight or in a dark room, being able to adjust the brightness and resolution of your screen ensures that you can always view content comfortably and clearly.

Adjusting Screen Brightness

Your Pixel 9a allows you to easily adjust the brightness of your screen for optimal viewing. To adjust the screen brightness:

1. Auto-Brightness:
   - The Pixel 9a has an Auto-Brightness feature that automatically adjusts the screen brightness based on your surroundings. This is useful if you want to conserve battery life and avoid manually adjusting the brightness. To enable or disable Auto-Brightness, follow these steps:
   - Go to Settings > Display.
   - Toggle Adaptive Brightness on or off.
      - The phone will automatically adjust brightness according to the lighting conditions around you.

2. Manual Brightness Adjustment:
   - If you prefer to manually control the brightness, swipe down the notification shade to access the Quick Settings panel. Here, you'll find a slider for Brightness that you can drag left or right to decrease or increase the brightness level.
   - You can also adjust it by going to Settings > Display > Brightness and manually adjusting the level to your preference.

Adjusting Display Resolution

While the Google Pixel 9a does not support a wide range of resolution adjustments like some high-end devices, it still offers an optimal display resolution that ensures crisp text and vibrant colors.

However, to conserve battery life, the phone dynamically adjusts the screen resolution based on usage, providing the best balance between performance and energy efficiency.

To check and adjust display settings, including any available resolution-related options:

1. Open Settings.
2. Navigate to Display > Advanced Settings.
3. While the Pixel 9a doesn't have a dedicated resolution slider, you can adjust other visual settings such as Screen Calibration for color accuracy and Ambient Display.

Setting Up Dark Mode and Themes

Many users prefer Dark Mode for its sleek appearance and the added benefit of reduced eye strain and battery savings, especially when using their device at night. Additionally, Google Pixel devices offer various themes to personalize your experience further.

Enabling Dark Mode

To enable Dark Mode on your Google Pixel 9a:

1. Open the Settings app.

2. Scroll down and select Display.

3. Choose Dark Theme, then toggle it on.

Once activated, the entire system interface—apps, settings, and Google apps like Google Photos, Gmail, and Google Assistant—will switch to a darker background with light text, making it easier on your eyes in low-light environments. Dark Mode also conserves battery life by reducing the energy used by OLED screens, which display dark pixels more efficiently.

Setting Up Custom Themes

In addition to Dark Mode, the Pixel 9a allows you to personalize your device further by adjusting the theme, accent colors, and wallpaper.

To customize your Pixel's theme:

1. Go to Settings.

2. Select Display.

3. Tap Styles & Wallpapers.

4. Choose Set a Style to pick a theme or accent color. You can choose from pre-configured styles or create your own by adjusting font, icon size, and color.

In the Styles & Wallpapers section, you can also change the wallpaper to personalize the device's look, or opt for Google's Live Wallpapers that offer dynamic, interactive backgrounds.

With these options, you can make your Pixel 9a truly yours, from the visuals to the feel of the device.

Managing Audio and Volume Settings

The audio on your Pixel 9a is designed to deliver clear and loud sound, whether you're watching videos, listening to music, or taking calls. Adjusting audio and volume settings ensures that you can achieve the perfect balance for your needs, whether in a noisy environment or a quiet room.

Adjusting Volume Settings

Your Pixel 9a allows you to adjust various volume levels to suit your audio needs:

1. **Ring Volume:** The ringtone and notifications volume can be adjusted using the volume buttons on the side of the phone. Pressing the volume button brings up a slider that lets you adjust the Ring volume, Media volume, and Alarm volume independently.

2. **Media Volume:** Use the same slider to adjust the volume for apps, games, music, and videos. You can fine-tune the sound for individual apps in Settings > Sound > Advanced.

3. Alarm Volume: Alarm volume is adjusted independently of other volume levels. You can set this to a higher level for better alerts during important times.

4. Do Not Disturb Mode: If you don't want to be disturbed by calls or notifications, the Do Not Disturb mode allows you to silence all or specific types of notifications. To enable it:
  - Swipe down on the notification shade.
  - Tap the Do Not Disturb icon to toggle it on or off.

You can further customize the Do Not Disturb settings by going to Settings > Sound > Do Not Disturb.

Using Sound Enhancements

To improve your audio experience, the Pixel 9a offers a range of audio enhancements, including stereo sound and adaptive sound features. These settings optimize the sound based on the content you're listening to and the environment.

1. Stereo Sound: The Pixel 9a is equipped with stereo speakers that provide a more immersive sound experience. To adjust this:
  - Go to Settings > Sound.
  - Enable Stereo Sound for better left-right sound separation, especially when watching movies or playing games.

2. Adaptive Sound: This feature adjusts the sound according to the ambient environment. If you're in a noisy place, the Pixel will automatically increase the sound quality to help you hear more clearly. To enable this:
- Go to Settings > Sound > Adaptive Sound.
- Toggle Adaptive Sound to on.

Using Bluetooth Audio

For a more private listening experience, or if you prefer to use wireless headphones, the Pixel 9a supports Bluetooth audio. To connect Bluetooth audio devices:

1. Open Settings.
2. Tap Bluetooth and turn it on.
3. Find and select your Bluetooth device from the list of available devices.
4. Once connected, you'll be able to stream audio directly to your Bluetooth headphones, speakers, or car system.

The Pixel 9a also supports aptX and AAC codecs for high-quality wireless audio.

Using Screen and Sound Enhancements

Your Pixel 9a is not just about regular display and audio settings—it also features advanced screen and sound enhancements that make your multimedia experience more dynamic.

Using Ambient Display

The Ambient Display feature allows you to see notifications, time, and other relevant information without unlocking your phone. This is particularly useful for quick glances at your device when it's resting on a table or nightstand.

To enable Ambient Display:

1. Open Settings.
2. Go to Display.
3. Toggle on Ambient Display.

With this feature activated, you'll see notifications, the time, and other details light up briefly on the screen when you receive new messages, calls, or other alerts.

Night Light

The Night Light feature helps reduce eye strain by applying a warm filter to the screen, which is easier on the eyes, especially during late-night use. To enable Night Light:

1. Open Settings > Display.
2. Toggle Night Light to on.
3. Adjust the intensity and schedule to turn it on and off automatically.

This feature is useful for users who enjoy reading or browsing the web at night and want to avoid blue light that may interfere with sleep.

Sound and Screen Sync for Videos

For a more immersive multimedia experience, you can enable sound and screen sync to ensure that the audio matches the visual cues while watching videos. Whether you're playing games or watching movies, this ensures a more fluid and synchronized experience.

1. Open the Settings app.
2. Go to Sound > Advanced.
3. Toggle Sound Synchronization to on.

This ensures that your audio and video play in perfect harmony, eliminating any lag or desynchronization.

Conclusion

Setting up your Google Pixel 9a to deliver the best possible display, audio, and visual experience involves fine-tuning settings to suit your personal preferences. By adjusting display brightness, enabling Dark Mode, and customizing themes, you can make your device more visually comfortable and energy-efficient. Meanwhile, by managing volume settings, using sound enhancements, and exploring screen and audio features, you can enjoy a more immersive multimedia experience. With these settings, your Pixel 9a can be perfectly tailored to provide the most satisfying customer experience.

Chapter 8: Personalization and Customization

One of the greatest advantages of owning a Google Pixel 9a is its ability to be tailored to your preferences. Whether you want to adjust how your home screen looks, organize apps, or personalize how notifications appear, the Google Pixel 9a offers a wide range of customization options to help you create a personalized and efficient user experience. This chapter will guide you through several key features to make your Pixel 9a truly your own. We'll cover how to customize the home screen, manage themes, wallpapers, and widgets, personalize notifications and quick settings, and utilize the Always-On Display and Ambient Display.

Customizing Your Pixel 9a's Home Screen

The **home screen** of your Google Pixel 9a is where you interact with apps and widgets, organize your tasks, and access important information. Personalizing the home screen can make your device more efficient and visually appealing, so it feels unique to you. Here's how you can customize your Pixel 9a's home screen:

Organizing Your Apps

You can organize apps on your home screen in a way that makes the most sense for you. Whether you prefer to keep everything on the first screen for easy access or organize your apps into folders, the Pixel 9a offers flexibility.

1. **Moving Apps**: To move an app to a different spot on the home screen, press and hold the app icon. Once the icon becomes draggable, drag it to your desired location. You can move apps to different pages on the home screen as well.

2. **Creating Folders**: If you have several apps of a similar type (e.g., social media apps), you can group them into folders to reduce clutter.

   - Press and hold an app icon until it becomes draggable.

   - Drag it over another app that you want to group it with.

   - A folder will automatically be created with both apps inside it.

   - You can then tap on the folder to rename it (e.g., "Social Media") or add more apps to it.

3. **Removing Apps from the Home Screen**: If you have apps that you no longer need or that you want to keep off the home screen for now, you can remove them without uninstalling them. Simply press and hold the app icon and drag it to the "Remove" area at the top of the screen. This will only remove the app from the home screen but will keep it in your app drawer.

4. **App Drawer**: To access all your installed apps, swipe up from the bottom of your home screen. Here, you'll find all of your apps organized alphabetically. If you prefer, you can enable a search bar at the top to quickly find the app you're looking for.

Home Screen Layout

To make the home screen more functional, you can change its layout and how apps appear. You can resize the app icons, change grid spacing, and choose how many rows and columns of icons are visible.

1. **Change Grid Size**: You can change the grid size for how apps are laid out. Go to **Settings** > **Display** > **Home screen** > **Grid**. From here, you can select between various grid sizes, allowing you to customize how many apps appear on each row and column.

2. **App Icon Size**: You can also adjust the size of the app icons. To do so, go to **Settings > Display > Home screen > Icon size**. This will give you a slider to increase or decrease the size of your app icons.

Managing Themes, Wallpapers, and Widgets

A key part of personalizing your Pixel 9a is choosing the right **themes**, **wallpapers**, and **widgets**. These elements allow you to express your style, create a sense of calm, and have at-a-glance information that is important to you.

Wallpapers

Changing your wallpaper is a simple way to refresh the look of your home screen. The Pixel 9a gives you plenty of options for customizing the background with different wallpapers:

1. **Setting a Wallpaper:**

   ○ Go to **Settings > Display > Wallpaper**.

   ○ Choose between **Live wallpapers** or **static wallpapers**. Live wallpapers offer dynamic, interactive visuals, while static wallpapers provide a traditional image.

- ○ You can pick from the default selection of wallpapers, or tap on **My Photos** to select a wallpaper from your gallery.

2. **Choosing a Live Wallpaper**:

- ○ For an added touch, Pixel 9a allows you to use **live wallpapers**, which provide animated visuals. Live wallpapers can change based on the time of day, weather, or other dynamic factors.

3. **Wallpaper Style**:

- ○ You can adjust the way your wallpaper is displayed (fit, crop, or stretch) to suit your device's screen resolution and personal preferences. Some live wallpapers will even change depending on how you interact with them.

Themes

The Pixel 9a allows you to further personalize the device by changing its **theme** to suit your preferred aesthetic. Themes adjust the colors and appearance of system UI elements, such as icons, buttons, and backgrounds.

1. **Dark Theme:** To enable **Dark Mode**, which is easier on the eyes at night and saves battery life, navigate to **Settings > Display > Theme**, and select **Dark**.

2. **Accent Colors:**

   ○ Go to **Settings > Display > Styles & Wallpapers**.

   ○ Here, you can choose from a selection of **accent colors** to alter the color of icons, highlights, and other UI elements. Whether you prefer vibrant hues or subtle shades, you can adjust the entire interface to match your personal style.

Widgets

Widgets allow you to add mini apps to your home screen for quick access to information like the weather, news, calendar events, and more. These widgets provide at-a-glance information, saving you the time of opening specific apps.

1. **Adding Widgets:**

   ○ To add a widget to your home screen, press and hold any open space on the screen.

- ○ Tap **Widgets** at the bottom of the screen.

- ○ Scroll through the available widgets and select one to add to your home screen.

- ○ Drag it to the desired spot on your home screen.

2. **Resizing Widgets**:

- ○ You can resize widgets to better fit your home screen layout. Simply press and hold the widget, and adjust the size by dragging the corners.

Personalizing Notifications and Quick Settings

Personalizing **notifications** and **quick settings** can help you streamline your Pixel 9a experience and ensure you receive only the information that matters most to you. Whether you want to organize notifications by priority or adjust quick settings for one-touch access, there's a lot you can do to create a more efficient and personalized interface.

Managing Notifications

Your Pixel 9a allows you to control how, when, and where notifications appear. You can prioritize which apps can send you notifications, silence unnecessary alerts, and customize how notifications are displayed.

1. **Customizing Notifications**:

   o Open **Settings** > **Apps & notifications** > **Notifications**.

   o From here, you can manage how notifications appear for different apps. You can choose whether an app shows notifications on the lock screen, displays notifications as pop-ups, or sends sound alerts.

2. **Prioritizing Notifications**:

   o If you want certain notifications to be more prominent, you can give them higher priority. Go to **Settings** > **Apps & notifications** > **Notifications** > **Advanced** > **Priority notifications**.

   o You can enable **Do Not Disturb** settings to suppress less important notifications, allowing only priority notifications to interrupt you.

3. **Silent Notifications**:

   ○ If you want to stop receiving sound alerts but still want to see notifications, you can set specific apps to **silent mode** by going into **App Notifications** and toggling the "silent" option.

Quick Settings Customization

The **Quick Settings** menu provides fast access to essential features like Wi-Fi, Bluetooth, airplane mode, and more. Personalizing this menu can save you time and make it more convenient to access the settings you use most often.

1. **Accessing Quick Settings**:

   ○ To access **Quick Settings**, swipe down from the top of the screen.

   ○ You will see icons for things like Wi-Fi, Bluetooth, Do Not Disturb, and more. To expand or collapse the menu, swipe up or down.

2. **Customizing Quick Settings**:

- To customize your Quick Settings, swipe down twice from the top of the screen and tap the **pencil icon** to enter the edit mode.

- Here, you can rearrange, add, or remove options based on your needs. For example, you can add a **Screenshot** shortcut or a **Battery Saver** toggle for quick access.

Using Always-On Display and Ambient Display

The **Always-On Display** and **Ambient Display** features are convenient ways to access important information without unlocking your phone. These features allow you to check notifications, time, and other key details with minimal effort.

Always-On Display (AOD)

The **Always-On Display** keeps certain information visible on your screen even when the device is in standby mode. It's an easy way to glance at your device without unlocking it. The Pixel 9a allows you to customize the Always-On Display to show different information, including notifications, time, and even your preferred wallpaper.

1. **Enabling Always-On Display**:

   ○ Go to **Settings** > **Display** > **Lock screen**.

   ○ Toggle the **Always-on display** switch to the **on** position.

   ○ The screen will now display important details, like the time and recent notifications, even when the device is locked.

2. **Customizing Always-On Display**: You can further customize what appears on your Always-On Display, such as enabling or disabling notifications, showing the clock in different formats, or even using a custom wallpaper.

Ambient Display

The **Ambient Display** feature allows you to view important details when you pick up your phone or when you receive notifications. This is different from Always-On Display in that it only activates when your phone senses movement or when notifications arrive.

1. **Enabling Ambient Display**:

- Go to **Settings** > **Display** > **Ambient display**.

- Enable the **Ambient display** option so that your phone's screen briefly lights up to show key information.

2. **Customizing Ambient Display**:

- You can choose what shows up on your screen, such as notifications, the time, or custom messages, depending on the actions you've set.

Conclusion

Personalizing your Google Pixel 9a allows you to create a device that truly reflects your style, preferences, and needs. Whether it's adjusting the home screen layout, selecting your ideal wallpaper, or managing notifications and quick settings, the Pixel 9a gives you full control over how your phone looks and functions. By using these customization options, you can ensure that your Pixel 9a not only looks great but also offers a streamlined, efficient user experience tailored to your lifestyle. With personalization features like Always-On Display, widgets, and dark mode, your Google Pixel 9a will work smarter, not harder, for you.

Chapter 9: Maintenance and Troubleshooting

Maintaining your Google Pixel 9a is crucial to keeping it running smoothly and ensuring that it continues to function optimally for as long as possible. Like any high-tech device, regular upkeep, software updates, and troubleshooting can prevent many issues and extend the life of your phone. In this chapter, we'll explore important tips for cleaning and caring for your Pixel 9a, how to keep your software up to date, and how to resolve common issues and errors. We'll also cover factory reset and recovery options, and give advice on troubleshooting connectivity and app problems.

Cleaning and Caring for Your Pixel 9a

Proper care and cleaning of your Pixel 9a are essential for maintaining its appearance and functionality. Over time, dirt, dust, and oil can accumulate on your device, which can affect the performance of buttons, screens, and ports. Additionally, consistent maintenance can help ensure that your phone stays in pristine condition, preventing unnecessary wear and tear.

Cleaning the Exterior

To maintain the external appearance of your Pixel 9a, use the following steps for cleaning:

1. **Screen Cleaning**:

    - Use a soft, lint-free microfiber cloth to clean the screen. Microfiber cloths are gentle on the screen and will not scratch the surface.

    - If necessary, lightly dampen the cloth with water or a screen-safe cleaner. Never apply liquid directly to the phone, as this can cause moisture damage.

    - Gently wipe the screen in a circular motion to remove smudges, fingerprints, and dust.

2. **Cleaning the Back and Sides**:

    - The back of the Pixel 9a is often a magnet for smudges and oils, particularly if the phone has a glass back. Use the same microfiber cloth to wipe down the back.

    - If your phone is in a case, be sure to remove the case occasionally to clean both the phone and the case itself. Cases can collect dust, and the buildup can be transferred to your phone.

3. **Ports and Speakers**:

   o Dust and debris can accumulate in the charging port, headphone jack, and speaker grills. To clean these areas, use a soft-bristled brush or a can of compressed air. Be gentle to avoid damaging the delicate internal components.

   o Avoid using metal objects or toothpicks, as they can damage the ports.

4. **Camera Lens**:

   o Your camera lens should also be cleaned regularly to maintain photo clarity. Use a microfiber cloth or lens cleaning solution designed specifically for cameras to gently clean the lens.

Caring for Your Pixel 9a

To further protect your Pixel 9a, consider the following care tips:

1. **Use a Case**:

    o A protective case can help protect your device from drops, scratches, and impacts. Choose a case that offers good shock absorption while allowing easy access to all ports and buttons.

    o If you're concerned about maintaining the appearance of your phone, consider a clear case that lets the design of the phone show while offering protection.

2. **Screen Protector**:

    o Applying a screen protector will help protect your phone's screen from scratches and minor impacts. Screen protectors come in various types, including tempered glass and plastic film, each offering varying levels of protection.

3. **Avoid Extreme Temperatures**:

    o Avoid leaving your Pixel 9a in extreme temperatures, such as in direct sunlight or in a hot car. Prolonged exposure to high or low temperatures can damage the battery and other internal components.

Updating Your Pixel 9a Software

Regular software updates are essential to keep your Pixel 9a secure, improve its performance, and introduce new features. Google frequently releases updates for the Pixel series, including security patches and bug fixes.

Enabling Automatic Updates

To make sure you are always up to date, enable automatic software updates on your Pixel 9a:

1. **Go to Settings > System > Software update**.

2. Enable the **Auto-download over Wi-Fi** option to ensure that updates are automatically downloaded when connected to Wi-Fi.

3. Enable **Install updates automatically** to allow updates to install in the background, minimizing interruptions.

Manually Checking for Updates

Sometimes, updates may not download automatically, or you may want to check for updates manually. To do so:

1. Go to **Settings** > **System** > **Software update**.

2. If an update is available, you will see a prompt to download and install it. Make sure your phone is connected to Wi-Fi and plugged into a charger before starting the update to avoid interruptions.

Benefits of Keeping Your Software Updated

- **Security**: Regular software updates ensure that your device has the latest security patches to protect against malware, vulnerabilities, and potential exploits.

- **Performance**: Software updates may improve your Pixel 9a's speed, efficiency, and overall performance by fixing bugs or optimizing system processes.

- **New Features**: Updates often bring new features, enhancements, and improvements to the user experience. These updates may include new gestures, UI tweaks, or even camera optimizations.

Resolving Common Issues and Errors

Like any electronic device, the Pixel 9a can sometimes encounter issues. While many issues can be resolved quickly, there are also a few simple troubleshooting steps you can take before seeking professional help.

Common Issues

1. **Phone Freezing or Lagging**:

   - **Cause**: Sometimes, apps or system processes can cause your Pixel 9a to freeze or lag.

   - **Solution**:

     - Close unused apps by opening the **Recent Apps** menu and swiping away the apps you don't need.

     - Restart your device. Hold the **Power** button until the power menu appears, and select **Restart**.

     - If the issue persists, check for software updates, as new updates may address performance issues.

2. **Battery Draining Too Quickly**:

   o **Cause**: Excessive background apps, screen brightness, or outdated software can contribute to faster battery drain.

   o **Solution**:

      ▪ Go to **Settings** > **Battery** and check which apps are using the most power. You can also enable **Battery Saver** mode to extend battery life.

      ▪ Lower screen brightness or enable **Adaptive brightness** to let the phone adjust brightness automatically.

      ▪ Turn off location services, Wi-Fi, or Bluetooth when not in use to conserve power.

3. **Wi-Fi or Bluetooth Not Connecting**:

   o **Cause**: Wi-Fi or Bluetooth issues may arise due to interference, incorrect settings, or outdated software.

- ○ **Solution**:

  - ■ Restart your router or Bluetooth device.

  - ■ Toggle the Wi-Fi or Bluetooth setting off and on again in the **Quick Settings** menu.

  - ■ Forget the network or Bluetooth device by going to **Settings** > **Wi-Fi** or **Bluetooth**, tapping the gear icon next to the network/device, and selecting **Forget**. Then, reconnect by selecting the network/device and entering any required credentials.

4. **App Crashes**:

   - ○ **Cause**: App crashes can be caused by bugs, outdated versions, or issues with the app's cache.

   - ○ **Solution**:

     - ■ Update the app through the **Google Play Store**.

     - ■ Clear the app's cache by going to **Settings** > **Apps** &

notifications > **See all apps**, selecting the app, and tapping **Storage** > **Clear Cache**.

Factory Reset and Recovery Options

If all else fails, or if your Pixel 9a is still experiencing persistent issues, a **factory reset** may be the solution. A factory reset will erase all data and settings on your phone and restore it to its original state.

Factory Reset

1. **Backup Your Data**: Before performing a factory reset, make sure to back up all your important data, including photos, contacts, and app data. You can use Google's **Google Drive** backup options or third-party cloud services for this.

2. **Factory Reset**:

   ○ Go to **Settings** > **System** > **Reset options** > **Erase all data (factory reset)**.

- Tap **Erase all data**, then confirm your action by tapping **Erase all**.

Note that a factory reset will delete all data from your device, so make sure to back everything up before proceeding.

Recovery Mode

If your Pixel 9a is unresponsive or unable to boot into the system, you can use the **recovery mode** to troubleshoot or perform a factory reset.

1. **Enter Recovery Mode:**

   - Turn off your Pixel 9a.

   - Press and hold the **Volume Down** button and the **Power** button simultaneously until the bootloader screen appears.

   - Use the **Volume** buttons to navigate to the **Recovery mode** option and press the **Power** button to select it.

   - From the recovery menu, you can perform a **Factory Reset** or try other options like **Wipe cache partition** to fix system issues without losing your data.

Troubleshooting Connectivity and App Issues

If you encounter issues with **Wi-Fi**, **Bluetooth**, or other connectivity options, or if your apps are not functioning properly, the following steps can help:

1. **Wi-Fi Issues**:

   o Ensure that your phone is connected to the correct Wi-Fi network.

   o Check if other devices are able to connect to the same Wi-Fi network to rule out network issues.

   o Reset your router or modem if needed.

2. **Bluetooth Problems**:

   o Ensure your Bluetooth device is in pairing mode and close to the Pixel 9a.

   o Clear the Bluetooth cache by going to **Settings** > **Apps & notifications** > **See all apps** > **Bluetooth** > **Storage** >

Clear Cache.

3. **App Issues**:

   ○ Update the app or reinstall it if it continues to crash or misbehave.

   ○ For specific issues, consult the app's **Help** section or contact the app developer for support.

Conclusion

Maintaining and troubleshooting your Google Pixel 9a is crucial for a smooth, long-lasting experience. Regularly cleaning your device, updating software, and resolving common issues proactively can help you avoid major problems. If necessary, factory reset and recovery options are available to restore your device to a working state. By following the steps in this chapter, you can ensure your Pixel 9a remains reliable and performs at its best for years to come.

Chapter 10: Advanced Features and Hidden Tips

Using Developer Options and Custom Settings

The Google Pixel 9a is packed with tools for everyday users, but under the hood, there's a wealth of advanced features waiting to be unlocked. For power users, developers, or even the curious tech enthusiast, **Developer Options** opens up a deeper level of control and customization.

Accessing Developer Options

To activate Developer Options on your Pixel 9a:

1. Open **Settings**.

2. Scroll down and tap **About phone**.

3. Find **Build number** and tap it **seven times**.

4. You'll be prompted to enter your device's PIN or unlock pattern.

5. After that, a new **Developer options** menu will appear under **System > Advanced**.

Once unlocked, you'll find a menu filled with powerful features. Here's how some of them can elevate your experience:

USB Debugging – This is essential if you plan to connect your device to a PC for tasks like rooting, using ADB commands, or developing Android apps.

Animation Scales – Reduce window and transition animation scales to make your phone feel faster and more responsive. Many users set these to 0.5x or turn them off altogether for snappier performance.

Force Dark Mode – Even if an app doesn't support dark mode, you can force it using this toggle. It helps save battery and is easier on the eyes.

Background Process Limit – You can limit how many background apps run, which is useful for optimizing performance or battery life, especially during travel or low battery situations.

Show Taps and Pointer Location – For those creating tutorials or screen recordings, enabling these features visually displays your touches and inputs.

Override Force-Enable Apps on External Storage – This is useful for moving apps to external storage (though not commonly needed with Pixel's internal storage and cloud sync).

Remember, while Developer Options are powerful, misusing them can affect performance or behavior. Always research changes you plan to make.

Gesture Navigation and Custom Shortcuts

The Pixel 9a takes navigation to a new level with **intuitive gestures** and customizable shortcuts, replacing old-fashioned buttons with swipes and taps.

Navigating with Gestures

To enable gesture navigation:

1. Go to **Settings** > **System** > **Gestures** > **System navigation**.

2. Select **Gesture navigation**.

Here are some core gestures:

- **Swipe up** from the bottom to go home.

- **Swipe up and hold** to open recent apps.

- **Swipe from the left or right edge** to go back.

- **Swipe diagonally from the bottom corners** to activate Google Assistant.

These gestures become second nature over time and allow for smoother multitasking.

One-Handed Mode

Pixel's gesture system also includes one-handed mode:

- Swipe down on the bottom edge to bring content lower on the screen – great for quick, top-reach access.

Enable it via: **Settings > System > Gestures > One-handed mode**.

Customizing Quick Gestures

Your Pixel includes additional gestures under **Settings > System > Gestures**, such as:

- **Quick Tap to Start Action** – Double tap the back of the phone to perform actions like launching apps, taking screenshots, or accessing Assistant.

- **Flip to Shhh** – Flip your phone face down to enable Do Not Disturb.

- **Press and hold power button for Assistant** – Access Google Assistant instantly.

These shortcuts save time and reduce steps. For example, setting Quick Tap to open your camera lets you never miss a spontaneous photo moment.

Third-Party Customization

Want more customization? Apps like **Button Mapper** or **Nova Launcher** offer even greater control over gestures and shortcuts, including double-tap-to-lock or swipe actions from any screen.

Advanced Battery Management Features

The Pixel 9a already boasts an impressive battery, but Google's adaptive system allows you to push battery life even further.

Adaptive Battery

Enabled by default, this feature uses machine learning to understand your usage habits. Apps you rarely use are limited in background activity to save power.

Find it under: **Settings > Battery > Adaptive preferences > Adaptive Battery**.

Battery Saver and Extreme Battery Saver

Battery Saver reduces performance, limits background activity, and disables visual effects. You can enable it manually or schedule it to turn on automatically at a specific percentage.

Extreme Battery Saver takes things further:

- Only essential apps are allowed.

- Notifications and background activity are paused.

- Performance is throttled to the minimum necessary.

This feature is a lifesaver during emergencies, travel, or long days out.

App Battery Usage and Restriction

See which apps are using the most battery via: **Settings > Battery > Battery usage**.

You can restrict heavy apps:

1. Tap the app.

2. Choose **Restricted** to prevent it from using battery in the background.

Battery Health Tips

- Use dark mode, especially with OLED displays.

- Avoid letting the battery drop below 20% regularly.

- Use the **Adaptive Charging** feature to protect battery longevity by slowly charging overnight.

- Keep software up to date – each update includes battery and performance tweaks.

Tips for Maximizing Device Performance

Performance optimization isn't just about speed—it's about getting the most consistent, smooth experience possible from your device.

Regularly Clear Cache

Apps like Chrome, Instagram, and Facebook can store massive cache data. Clear this periodically: **Settings > Storage > Apps > [App Name] > Clear Cache**.

Limit Background Apps

Background apps can drain memory and battery. Enable **Developer Options** and reduce the number of allowed background processes, or use Digital Wellbeing to identify overuse.

Reboot Weekly

A simple weekly restart helps clear temporary files, reset RAM, and resolve minor bugs. Think of it as a refresh for your Pixel.

Uninstall Unused Apps

Keeping unnecessary apps can clog memory and slow down processes. Clean up every few weeks: **Settings > Apps > See all apps**.

Use Lite Versions of Apps

Many major apps offer "lite" versions – Facebook Lite, Messenger Lite, YouTube Go – which consume fewer resources and still offer essential functions.

Keep Software Updated

Google regularly pushes updates not just for security, but performance enhancements too. Go to: **Settings > System > System update**.

Widgets and Live Wallpapers

Too many widgets or animated backgrounds may slow your device. Stick to static wallpapers and essential widgets for best performance.

Exploring Accessibility Features

Google Pixel 9a's **Accessibility** suite is designed to make the phone inclusive and easier for all users, including those with vision, hearing, or mobility challenges.

Vision Assistance

- **Magnification** – Temporarily magnify content with a three-finger tap or shortcut.

- **Color correction and inversion** – Help users with color blindness or vision sensitivity.

- **Font size and Display size** – Scale text and elements to make content more readable.

- **TalkBack** – A screen reader for blind or visually impaired users. Navigate with spoken feedback.

Hearing Support

- **Live Caption** – Instantly adds subtitles to videos, podcasts, and audio messages—even without internet.

- **Sound Amplifier** – Enhances audio from your surroundings when using headphones.

- **Real-time Transcribe** – Converts speech into text for those with hearing loss.

Mobility Aids

- **Switch Access** – Control your phone using a switch device instead of the touchscreen.

- **Voice Access** – Navigate using voice commands; great for limited mobility.

- **Interaction Controls** – Delay touch response, ignore repeated taps, or limit gesture sensitivity.

Custom Accessibility Shortcuts

You can add shortcuts to your power menu or navigation bar for quick access: **Settings > Accessibility > Accessibility Menu**.

Digital Wellbeing Integration

The accessibility features also tie into Digital Wellbeing tools, which support focus and screen time control. These features make using the phone healthier, especially for individuals prone to eye strain, distraction, or fatigue.

Chapter 11: Security and Privacy Settings

Security and privacy are among the most important aspects of smartphone ownership in today's digitally connected world. The Google Pixel 9a is built with a strong foundation of security tools and privacy-focused settings that put you in control of your data, your personal information, and how your phone is accessed. From biometric authentication to app-level permissions and two-factor authentication, this chapter will walk you through the essential features and settings to ensure your Pixel 9a is protected — while delivering a smooth, satisfying, and user-centric experience.

Managing Your Google Account Security

Your Google Account is the backbone of your Pixel 9a experience. It syncs your apps, email, contacts, calendar, photos, and even your payment methods. That's why it's vital to keep this account secure.

Accessing Security Settings

To begin managing your Google Account security:

1. Open **Settings** on your Pixel 9a.

2. Scroll down and tap **Google**.

3. Tap **Manage your Google Account**.

4. Swipe to the **Security** tab at the top.

From this screen, you can review and adjust your security settings.

Important Security Tools

1. Security Check-Up: Google provides a **Security Check-Up** tool that reviews your account's safety. It checks for suspicious logins, outdated recovery information, unused devices, and third-party apps with access. It's a fast and easy way to tighten your digital security.

2. Recovery Information: Ensure your **recovery email and phone number** are up to date. These are essential if you ever need to recover your Google Account or verify your identity when logging in from a new device.

3. Suspicious Activity Alerts: Under the **Recent security activity** section, you can review any unfamiliar sign-ins. If something looks suspicious, you'll have the option to take immediate action by changing your password or revoking device access.

4. Managing Devices: Scroll to **Your devices** to view all the devices that are currently signed in with your Google account. If you see a device you don't recognize, tap on it and choose **Sign out** to revoke access.

Maintaining control of your Google Account is essential, as it holds the keys to everything from your emails to Google Drive files and Google Pay transactions.

Setting Up Fingerprint and Face Recognition

Biometric authentication adds an extra layer of security and convenience. With the Pixel 9a, you can unlock your phone, approve app logins, and authorize purchases using just your fingerprint or facial recognition.

Setting Up Fingerprint Unlock

1. Open **Settings**.

2. Tap **Security** > **Fingerprint Unlock**.

3. You'll be prompted to set up a screen lock (if you haven't already).

4. Follow the on-screen instructions to scan your fingerprint.

5. Once complete, you can use your fingerprint to unlock your phone, verify Google Play purchases, or sign into apps.

Pro Tip: Register more than one fingerprint for convenience — such as both thumbs or your dominant index finger.

Setting Up Face Recognition

The Pixel 9a also supports face unlock for faster access.

1. Go to **Settings** > **Security** > **Face Unlock**.

2. Follow the instructions to allow your phone to scan your face.

Face Unlock is best used in well-lit environments. It's optimized for convenience rather than strict security — for example, it may not be as secure as fingerprint unlock for sensitive actions like authorizing payments.

Note: Face unlock on the Pixel 9a uses the front-facing camera, not infrared sensors, so while it's useful, it should be paired with a stronger form of authentication for banking and security-sensitive apps.

Securing Your Device with Screen Lock Options

Setting a screen lock is your first line of defense in preventing unauthorized access to your phone and data. Pixel 9a offers several screen lock methods, allowing you to choose one based on your preferred balance of security and convenience.

Screen Lock Options

1. **Swipe** – No security, for convenience only.

2. **Pattern** – A custom gesture on a 3x3 grid.

3. **PIN** – A 4- to 6-digit numerical code.

4. **Password** – A strong alphanumeric password.

5. **Fingerprint/Face Unlock** – Biometric options as discussed earlier.

To set or change your screen lock:

- Go to **Settings** > **Security** > **Screen lock** and choose your desired method.

Smart Lock: You can also set up Smart Lock to keep your phone unlocked in trusted situations — such as when you're home, when it's connected to a trusted Bluetooth device, or when it detects that you're carrying it.

To enable Smart Lock:

- Go to **Settings** > **Security** > **Advanced Settings** > **Smart Lock**.

This balances convenience with protection, letting you stay secure without frequent unlock interruptions when you're in a trusted environment.

Privacy Settings for Location, Camera, and Microphone

With increased awareness about data privacy, Android 14 on the Pixel 9a gives you granular control over which apps can access your camera, microphone, and location — and when.

Managing Location Permissions

1. Go to **Settings** > **Location**.

2. Tap **App location permissions** to view which apps are using your location.

3. For each app, you can choose:

   ○ **Allow all the time**

   ○ **Allow only while using the app**

   ○ **Deny**

Quick Tip: Use "Allow only while using the app" for apps like Maps or Uber. This ensures they can only access your location when you're actively using them.

Camera and Microphone Access

1. Go to **Settings** > **Privacy** > **Permission Manager**.

2. Choose **Camera** or **Microphone**.

3. Review which apps have access and set permissions accordingly.

Android now also includes a **privacy dashboard**, which provides a real-time view of how often apps are accessing sensitive data and sensors.

Indicator Icons

When an app is using your camera or microphone, your Pixel 9a will show a small green dot in the top-right corner of the screen. This transparency gives you peace of mind and immediate awareness.

You can even revoke all app access to the microphone and camera from **Quick Settings** with the toggles "Mic access" and "Camera access."

Using Two-Factor Authentication

Even with strong passwords, online accounts are vulnerable without an additional layer of protection. That's where **two-factor authentication (2FA)** — also known as two-step verification — comes in.

With 2FA enabled, even if someone has your password, they can't access your account without the second form of verification.

How to Enable 2FA on Your Google Account

1. Go to **myaccount.google.com/security**.

2. Scroll to the **Signing in to Google** section.

3. Tap **2-Step Verification** and follow the steps to set it up.

You can choose from several second-step options:

- **Google Prompt** (recommended): When you sign in, a prompt will appear on your Pixel 9a asking if you're trying to log in.

- **Backup Codes**: Use one-time codes if you're traveling or can't access your device.

- **Authenticator App**: Use apps like Google Authenticator or Authy to generate time-sensitive codes.

- **Security Key**: Physical hardware keys like a USB or NFC token (advanced users).

Tip: Always set up backup methods in case you lose access to your phone. Google allows you to store multiple methods, including recovery codes and backup email addresses.

Final Thoughts

Security and privacy are no longer optional in today's digital landscape — they are essential. The Google Pixel 9a provides you with advanced tools and intuitive controls to manage both with ease. By setting up strong screen locks, enabling biometric authentication, managing app permissions, using two-factor authentication, and staying vigilant about your account's activity, you can feel confident in your digital safety.

The real power of the Pixel 9a lies in how it empowers you to protect your information without making the experience frustrating or complicated. Every control is designed with usability in mind — because being secure should never come at the cost of a smooth and satisfying user experience.

Chapter 12: Updates and System Management

The performance, security, and longevity of your Google Pixel 9a are heavily reliant on regular system maintenance and updates. Thankfully, Google has designed this process to be as intuitive and stress-free as possible. Whether you're a seasoned Android user or brand new to smartphones, this chapter will walk you through the essentials of keeping your Pixel 9a in top shape — from software updates and app management to system backups and recovery options.

Checking for Software Updates

Keeping your Pixel 9a up to date ensures that you benefit from the latest features, improved performance, and critical security patches. Google provides monthly software updates and major Android version upgrades directly to Pixel devices — making them among the first to receive new features and security enhancements.

Why Updates Matter

Every software update from Google includes:

- **Security patches** to fix vulnerabilities.

- **Performance improvements** for smoother and faster operation.

- **Bug fixes** to resolve known issues.

- **Feature enhancements** to improve functionality or introduce new tools.

Your Pixel 9a is designed to check for these updates automatically, but you can always manually check to ensure you're on the latest version.

How to Check for Updates Manually

1. **Open Settings** on your Pixel 9a.

2. Scroll down and tap **System**.

3. Select **System update**.

4. Tap **Check for update**.

If an update is available, you'll be prompted to download and install it. Depending on the update size, this process can take a few minutes to over an hour. Make sure your phone is connected to Wi-Fi and plugged into a charger if your battery is below 50%.

Scheduled Updates and Smart Install

To minimize disruption, your Pixel 9a will often schedule updates to install **overnight** while your phone is idle and charging. This ensures you wake up to a freshly updated device without having to wait during your day.

Tip: You can delay the installation temporarily if you're in the middle of something critical — but don't wait too long, as security updates are essential for keeping your phone safe.

Managing System and App Updates

Beyond just the Android operating system, your Pixel 9a keeps dozens of built-in apps updated in the background. These updates are primarily delivered through the **Google Play Store** and **Google Play system updates** — a feature that allows parts of the OS to be updated without a full system reboot.

Keeping System Apps Updated

1. **Open the Google Play Store**.

2. Tap your profile icon in the top right corner.

3. Tap **Manage apps & device**.

4. Under **Updates available**, tap **Update all** or select individual apps to update.

System apps like Google Maps, Gmail, and the Pixel Launcher receive frequent updates to improve performance and add features. Keeping these apps current ensures your device runs smoothly and securely.

Managing Auto-Updates

If you'd prefer more control over when and how apps update:

- Go to **Play Store > Settings > Network preferences > Auto-update apps**.

- Choose between:

    o **Over any network**

    o **Over Wi-Fi only**

    o **Don't auto-update apps**

You might prefer to restrict updates to Wi-Fi to save on mobile data or disable auto-updates completely if you want to read reviews before installing new versions.

Google Play System Updates

These are under-the-hood enhancements to Android components like security libraries and media frameworks. To manually check for these:

1. Go to **Settings** > **Security**.

2. Scroll to **Google Play system update**.

3. Tap to check and install if available.

These updates don't usually require a full reboot and can enhance device safety without you even noticing.

Understanding Google Pixel 9a System Backups

A reliable backup system is your safety net in case you lose your device, experience a system failure, or upgrade to a new phone. Your Pixel 9a integrates deeply with Google's cloud backup features, making it easy to protect and recover your data.

What Gets Backed Up Automatically

When backup is enabled, Google saves the following:

- **Apps and app data**

- **Call history**

- **Device settings** (Wi-Fi passwords, wallpapers, language preferences, etc.)

- **SMS messages**

- **Photos and videos** (via Google Photos, if configured)

To ensure backup is enabled:

1. Open **Settings** > **System** > **Backup**.

2. Confirm **Backup by Google One** is turned on.

You can also see the last backup date and force a manual backup by tapping **Back up now**.

Google Photos: Unlimited Backup

Pixel 9a users can use **Google Photos** to back up images and videos in **high quality**, ensuring your memories are safe even if your phone is damaged or lost.

- Open the **Photos app** > tap your profile photo > **Photos settings** > **Back up & sync**.

- Turn on **Back up & sync** and choose your backup quality (original or storage saver).

Tip: Use Wi-Fi-only backups if you want to conserve mobile data.

Factory Reset and Data Recovery

Sometimes you need to start over — whether you're selling your phone, passing it on, or encountering an issue that can't be resolved with regular troubleshooting. That's where the **factory reset** and **data recovery** features come into play.

Performing a Factory Reset

A factory reset wipes all your personal data and settings, returning your Pixel 9a to its out-of-the-box state. This is an important step before trading or selling the device.

To reset:

1. Open **Settings**.

2. Tap **System > Reset options**.

3. Select **Erase all data (factory reset)**.

4. Follow the prompts to confirm.

Warning: This process deletes all data on your phone — make sure to back up everything you want to keep before proceeding.

Recovering Your Data

Once reset, you can recover your previous settings and data during the initial device setup:

- When prompted, select **Restore from Google Backup** and log in with the same Google Account.

- Choose the most recent backup to restore your apps, settings, and messages.

If you've used Google Photos and Google Drive, your media and files will automatically be available once you sign in.

Factory Reset Protection (FRP)

Pixel devices include **FRP** to prevent unauthorized access. If someone factory resets your phone without your permission, they'll be prompted to log in with your previously synced Google Account. This helps protect your data even if your device is stolen.

Important: Always remove your Google Account (via **Settings > Accounts**) before performing a factory reset if you plan to sell or give away your device.

Final Thoughts

The Google Pixel 9a is engineered to stay fast, secure, and up-to-date — and when you understand how to manage its updates and backups effectively, you unlock the full potential of your device. From seamless updates and smart cloud backups to safe reset and recovery tools, you have everything needed to keep your phone in peak condition.

By staying proactive with your system management, you not only extend the lifespan of your Pixel 9a but also enjoy the peace of mind that comes with knowing your personal data is secure, backed up, and ready to restore at a moment's notice.

Conclusion

Wrapping Up: Maximizing Your Pixel 9a Experience

By now, you've explored virtually every feature, function, and setting that makes the Google Pixel 9a a powerful tool in your hands. This isn't just a smartphone—it's a personal assistant, an entertainment hub, a professional-grade camera, a navigation system, and a digital vault. But even with all this technology at your fingertips, it's how you use it that truly defines your experience.

So let's recap, reflect, and expand on how to **maximize your Pixel 9a experience**—not just as a user but as someone who relies on this device for day-to-day convenience, creativity, communication, and more.

Make It Yours: Full Customization

The Pixel 9a offers deep levels of customization, so your phone truly reflects **your personality and lifestyle**:

- **Themes, Wallpapers, and Widgets** let you create a home screen that feels like your own.

- Adjusting **quick settings** allows fast access to the features you use most.

- Take advantage of **ambient and always-on displays** to keep essential info like time, notifications, and battery visible at a glance.

Don't stop at the basics—explore the **Pixel Tips app**, built right into your device, which offers helpful walkthroughs, suggestions, and feature highlights tailored to your usage patterns.

Stay Updated and Secure

Never underestimate the importance of software updates. Not only do they keep your device **safe from threats**, but they also unlock **new features** over time. With monthly security patches and regular Android version upgrades, the Pixel 9a stays fresh and responsive for years.

Security tools like **fingerprint unlock, facial recognition, two-factor authentication**, and **Google's privacy dashboard** ensure that your data remains yours. Customize these features so you never have to sacrifice ease of use for safety.

Embrace Google Services for Productivity

The tight integration of Google services like **Gmail, Calendar, Drive, Meet, and Keep** transforms your Pixel 9a into a mobile productivity suite. Whether you're scheduling a meeting, editing a document, or organizing your grocery list, these tools offer **cloud-based continuity** that travels with you across devices.

Use **Google Assistant** regularly to streamline tasks: set reminders, navigate hands-free, or even control smart home devices. The more you use it, the smarter and more useful it becomes.

Explore Advanced Features

If you've read through the Advanced Features and Hidden Tips chapter, you now know how much **potential lies beneath the surface**. From **gesture navigation** and **developer options** to **battery health management** and **performance optimization**, you've got a device that adapts to your needs.

Try new gestures like flip-to-shhh, one-handed mode, or screen pinning. Customize them to match your usage style. And don't be afraid to explore—many features are tucked away in submenus waiting to be discovered.

Take Care of Your Device

A device this powerful deserves good maintenance. Use the guide's cleaning tips, troubleshoot issues early, and use cloud backups to prevent data loss. When it's well cared for, the Pixel 9a rewards you with years of reliable performance.

In short, your Pixel 9a isn't just about what's in it—it's about what you do with it. Treat it as your trusted daily companion, and it will deliver value far beyond its specs.

Helpful Resources and Support Options

No matter how confident or tech-savvy you become with your Pixel 9a, there will be moments when you need support, answers, or just a deeper understanding of your device's capabilities. Google has built an excellent support ecosystem for its Pixel line, combining in-app guidance with online resources and community forums.

Here's where to turn when you need help, inspiration, or education:

The Pixel Tips App

Preloaded on your device, **Pixel Tips** is an interactive tool that walks you through new features, hidden tricks, and essential how-tos. If you skipped it during setup, don't worry—you can launch it anytime by searching "Tips" in the app drawer.

- Short, bite-sized tutorials

- Personalized recommendations based on your device usage

- Regular updates as new features are added

Google Support Website

The **Google Pixel Support Center** is your official hub for device support:

https://support.google.com/pixelphone

There, you'll find:

- Step-by-step troubleshooting guides

- Instructional videos

- FAQs on every Pixel model and Android version

- Details on warranty coverage and device repairs

If you're a reader who prefers self-service learning, this resource is constantly updated and very reliable.

YouTube Tutorials and Demos

Google's **official YouTube channel** for Pixel provides engaging video content for visual learners. You'll find walkthroughs on everything from using your Pixel camera like a pro to configuring battery optimization settings.

Search for: "Google Pixel 9a tutorials" or "Pixel tips & tricks"

Reddit and Pixel Enthusiast Forums

Sometimes, community-based advice is the most helpful. Reddit's **r/GooglePixel** subreddit is full of real-world users who share experiences, solve problems, and give honest reviews of features and apps.

Look for:

- Unofficial troubleshooting hacks

- User-recommended apps

- Feature usage tips not covered in official documents

Just keep in mind: community advice should always be cross-checked with Google's documentation for safety and accuracy.

Contacting Google Support and Community Forums

While self-help is effective for many users, sometimes you'll need **direct interaction with a human**. Whether you're facing a technical issue or need help setting something up, Google's support channels are fast, responsive, and global.

Live Chat and Phone Support

Visit support.google.com/pixelphone and scroll down to the **"Contact Us"** section. You'll usually have the following options:

- **Live Chat**: Chat with a support specialist within minutes. Ideal for quick fixes and feature questions.

- **Phone Call**: You can request a callback from a Google support agent.

- **Email Support**: For issues that are not urgent or that require attachments (screenshots, error logs).

Support is typically available **24/7**, especially in major English-speaking regions, and you can often choose your preferred language.

Google One Support

If you're a Google One subscriber, you get **priority support** for your Pixel device, along with storage perks and premium editing tools in Google Photos.

To access:

- Open the **Google One app**

- Tap **Support** and choose **Phone**, **Chat**, or **Email**

This level of support often includes advanced troubleshooting and personalized help.

Pixel Community Forum

Google's own Pixel Help Community is another excellent way to connect with other users and experts:

https://support.google.com/pixelphone/community

Browse topics, post questions, or join discussions. Often, Google product experts (marked with badges) respond to inquiries and share insight into known issues or features being rolled out.

Final Thoughts

Your journey with the Google Pixel 9a doesn't end here—it **evolves with you**. Whether you're just getting comfortable or diving deep into developer tools, this device is built to adapt, learn, and grow alongside your needs. By keeping your phone updated, backed up, and personalized to your lifestyle, you ensure it will always deliver peak performance.

But more importantly, you now have the **knowledge and confidence** to explore everything your Pixel can do—and to solve problems or find answers quickly when you need them.

Enjoy the experience, keep learning, and don't hesitate to reach out to Google's excellent support network when the time comes. Your Pixel 9a is more than just a phone—it's a partner in your digital life.